The New Glue:
How Politics is Replacing Religion — and What Comes Next for Humanity

The New Glue:
How Politics is Replacing Religion — and What Comes Next for Humanity

Rex Nihilo

Copyright Page

Title: *The New Glue: How Politics is Replacing Religion — and What Comes Next for Humanity*
Author: *Rex Nihilo*

Copyright © 2025 by Rex Nihilo
All rights reserved.

No part of this book may be reproduced, distributed, or transmitted in any form or by any means—including photocopying, recording, or other electronic or mechanical methods—without the prior written permission of the publisher, except in the case of brief quotations embodied in critical reviews and certain other noncommercial uses permitted by copyright law.

For information, permission requests, or media inquiries, contact:
Quite Frank Educational Services
Richmond, BC, Canada

Cover design by the author.
Printed in the United States of America.

ISBN: 978-1-997668-52-7

Library and Archives Canada Cataloguing in Publication Data pending.

Publisher's Note

This book represents the author's independent research and reflection. The opinions expressed are those of the author and do not necessarily reflect the views of Quite Frank Educational Services or any affiliated organization.

The New Glue: How Politics Replaced Religion — and What Comes Next for Humanity

Rex Nihilo

Introduction 1

Chapter 1: The Age of Belief — How Religion Held Humanity Together 3

    Part I: The Birth of the Sacred: From Tribal Myths to Civilization 3

    Part II: Gods, Empires, and the Architecture of Faith 8

Chapter 2: Philosophy and the Birth of Rational Community 15

    Part I: From Mythos to Logos — The Philosophical Revolution 15

    Part II: Ethics Without Gods — Building Societies on Reason 21

Chapter 3: The Scientific Revolution — Unraveling the Sacred Fabric 29

    Part I: The Fall of the Cosmic Order 29

    Part II: Enlightenment and the Machinery of Truth 36

Chapter 4: The Enlightenment and the Rise of the Individual 43

    Part I: Freedom, Reason, and the Death of Kings 43

    Part II: The Birth of Secular Morality 50

Chapter 5: The Nation-State — Politics Becomes the New Faith 57

    Part I: Nationalism as a Modern Religion...57

    Part II: The Myth of the People — Flags, Borders, and Belief 64

Chapter 6: The 20th Century — Ideologies as Modern Religions 71

    Part I: The Totalitarian Temptation — Communism and Fascism.........71

    Part II: Democracy's Faith — Liberty and the Myth of Progress...........78

Chapter 7: The Digital Age — Algorithms of Belief and Division 85

    Part I: The Network as the New Temple 85

Part II: The Algorithmic Gospel — Data, Desire, and the Manufacture of Meaning..................92

Chapter 8 – The Global Mind — Culture, Art, and the Post-Human Imagination 99

Part I – The Networked Imagination: Culture in the Age of Everywhere .99

Part II – The Post-Human Imagination: Technology, Consciousness, and the Future of Meaning 105

Chapter 9 – Science, Reason, and the Crisis of Meaning..................113

Part I – The Triumph of the Rational Mind 113

Part II – The Vacuum of the Soul: Can Science Satisfy the Heart?..................119

Chapter 10 – Technology, Power, and the New Gods of the 21st Century.127

Part I – Silicon Prophets: The Ideology of Innovation..................127

Part II – Techno-Faith: Immortality, AI, and the Quest for Transcendence 133

Chapter 11 – Globalization and the Search for a Shared Story..................141

Part I — The Fractured Planet and the Unfinished Human..................141

Part II — Toward a Planetary Language of Connection..................147

Chapter 12 — Beyond Earth: Humanity's Expansion and the Meaning of the Frontier..................155

Part I — The Frontier as Mirror: Exploration, Empire, and the Dream of the Infinite 155

Part II: "The Cosmic Covenant: Consciousness, Responsibility, and the Future of Humanity" 164

Chapter 13 — The Next Humanity: The Evolution of Consciousness..................175

Part I: "The Evolution of Consciousness: From Instinct to Insight"..................175

Part II: The Birth of the Inner Frontier: Consciousness, Compassion, and the Architecture of the Next Human 186

CHAPTER 14 — Integration: The Synthetic Horizon: AI, Meaning, and the Future of Intelligence 199

PART I — The Rise of the Synthetic Other: The New Landscape of the Mind 199

Chapter 15 — The Covenant of Meaning: What Humanity Owes the Future
....227

Part I — The Long Now: Responsibility, Meaning, and the Soul of a Species 227

Part II: The Testament of Tomorrow: Crafting a Civilizational Philosophy for the Next Humanity 237

THEMATIC BRIDGE — FROM FRACTURE TO FORM 249

EPILOGUE — THE QUIET WORK AHEAD..................................251

Bibliography 255

Glossary of Key Terms..259

Disclaimer & Acknowledgement of AI-Assisted Tools

This book is intended for educational and informational purposes only. The views and perspectives expressed herein reflect the author's interpretation of historical, philosophical, psychological, and cultural ideas and are not intended as professional, legal, medical, or psychological advice.

While this work explores themes related to politics, religion, technology, psychology, and social change, it does so from a reflective and analytical perspective. Readers are encouraged to engage critically with the material and to seek qualified professional guidance where appropriate.

Acknowledgement of AI-Assisted Tools

The author acknowledges the use of artificial intelligence–assisted tools, including OpenAI's ChatGPT, during the research, editing, and structural development of this book.

These tools were used to:

- assist with organizing complex ideas and themes,
- support research synthesis across multiple disciplines,
- refine language, clarity, and narrative flow,
- and help structure extended philosophical and conceptual arguments.

All final content, interpretations, perspectives, and conclusions are the responsibility of the author. AI tools were used as collaborative assistants and research aids, not as independent authors or sources of original insight.

The author affirms that this work represents a human-guided creative and intellectual process, shaped by lived experience, judgment, and intentional authorship.

"Until you make the unconscious conscious, it will direct your life and you will call it fate."

Carl Jung

"Homo sapiens is a storytelling animal that thinks in stories rather than in numbers or graphs."

Yuval Noah Harari

"We are not human beings having a spiritual experience; we are spiritual beings having a human experience."

Pierre Teilhard de Chardin

"You are an aperture through which the universe is looking at and exploring itself."

Alan Watts

"The world is not a problem waiting to be solved, but a reality waiting to be experienced."

Iain McGilchrist

Introduction

For tens of thousands of years, humanity has relied on stories to survive. Before there were nations or governments, before cities and markets, there were **shared myths** — ideas that bound people together, shaped moral systems, and created collective identity. Religion and philosophy were not merely intellectual exercises; they were the invisible architecture of civilization itself.

When a tribe believed in a common set of gods, or when an empire rallied around a divine emperor, every individual felt connected to something greater than themselves. Whether through the worship of Zeus, Yahweh, Allah, or the ancestral spirits of the forest, religion gave people an **answer to the chaos** of life: *Why are we here? What is right and wrong? To whom do we belong?*

This spiritual glue held societies together through countless centuries of change. When philosophers began to question divine authority — from Confucius and Buddha to Socrates and Marcus Aurelius — they didn't destroy the glue, they **refined it**. Philosophy replaced the mystical with the rational, the divine with the ethical. Humanity's sense of belonging evolved from shared gods to shared reason.

But then came science — and the story began to unravel.

The Scientific Revolution, while liberating in its discoveries, fractured the old narratives. For the first time, humanity learned that the Earth was not the center of the universe, that species evolved through natural processes, that the cosmos operated by laws of physics, not divine will. Science replaced myth with mechanism, faith with fact. And though this gave us extraordinary power, it also robbed us of certainty.

The question "What is true?" became answerable. But the question "Why does it matter?" became more elusive.

As religion retreated from public life, **politics rushed in to fill the void**. The Enlightenment produced new secular creeds — liberty, equality, fraternity — and new forms of collective belonging: nations, ideologies, and political movements. Instead of priests, we had politicians; instead of holy texts, we had constitutions and manifestos; instead of worship, we had civic ritual and patriotic pride.

By the 20th century, politics had become **the new religion of the masses**. Millions devoted their lives, even sacrificed them, for ideologies promising salvation: communism, fascism, liberal democracy. Each offered moral certainty, a sense of belonging, and a clear story of good and evil.

Yet, as we entered the 21st century, something shifted again. The world became too interconnected, too complex, too information-rich for traditional politics to hold it all together. Digital technology and social media, once celebrated as tools of democracy, fragmented the public sphere into countless echo chambers. Politics, once a unifying force for nations, now **divides families, friends, and entire cultures**.

We are left in a strange limbo — more connected than ever, yet more divided; more informed, yet less certain; freer, yet often emptier inside. Science has given us understanding, but not purpose. Politics gives us identity, but not peace.

So what comes next?

This book seeks to trace the story of how humanity moved from **shared myth to fractured ideology**, from **spiritual community to political tribe**, and what might lie beyond the current age of polarization. Could we be on the verge of a new kind of unity — one rooted not in dogma or ideology, but in shared humanity and planetary consciousness?

In exploring this question, we will look backward to the great civilizations of the past, inward to the human need for meaning, and forward to the possibilities of technology, science, and ethics in reshaping our collective destiny.

The glue that once bound us is cracking — but perhaps, in its place, a new adhesive is forming: a global understanding of what it means to be human in an age where truth, belief, and identity are being rewritten.

Chapter 1: The Age of Belief — How Religion Held Humanity Together

Part I: The Birth of the Sacred: From Tribal Myths to Civilization

Long before the first city rose or the first empire spread its banners across the earth, humans huddled around fires beneath star-choked skies, telling stories. Those stories — of spirits, ancestors, beasts, and gods — were not mere entertainments. They were blueprints for survival. They taught who we were, what was right and wrong, and why the world was as it was. From these whispered tales was born the sacred — a vast invisible web of meanings that bound small, vulnerable human groups into communities capable of enduring across generations.

To understand the emergence of religion is to understand the first social technology — the original operating system of human cooperation.

The Dawn of Sacred Consciousness

The earliest humans lived in a universe that was unpredictable and often cruel. Droughts, predators, and disease struck without pattern. Yet the human mind, wired to seek causation, began to find meaning in chaos. The rustling of grass became a spirit's whisper; thunder was the anger of the sky; death, a passage to another world. Anthropologists such as Mircea Eliade and Émile Durkheim observed that early religion was not a primitive form of science — it was a *response to vulnerability*.

Sacred thought turned random events into stories of intention. In those stories, humans were no longer powerless. They could pray, sacrifice, or appease; they could *negotiate* with existence itself. This impulse — to find order in disorder — is arguably the defining trait of our species.

Over time, those proto-religious intuitions gave rise to a powerful new social force: **shared belief**. A tribe that believed in the same spirit-world could trust one another beyond blood relations. The invisible gods became guarantors of promises. "If you cheat me," one might think, "the spirits will punish you." Religion thus created moral oversight before any human police or judge existed.

The anthropologist Pascal Boyer calls this the "supernatural monitoring hypothesis." Simply put, gods made humans behave. In evolutionary terms, belief in watchful deities offered a survival advantage — tribes that could trust each other cooperated better, hunted better, and defended themselves better.

The Power of Shared Myth

As language and symbolic thought developed, the earliest myths crystallized. They explained not only the natural world but social norms: how to marry, trade, fight, and die. Every ritual reinforced a group's cohesion. To dance the same dance or chant the same prayer was to feel the pulse of the tribe as one organism.

For hunter-gatherers, the sacred was everywhere — animism infused the forest, rivers, and animals with spirit. Totems and fetishes embodied the tribe's connection to nature. This wasn't superstition in the modern sense; it was **ecological intelligence expressed through story**. Seeing the divine in every aspect of the environment encouraged respect for natural cycles.

Over millennia, these patterns of thought became more elaborate. By the time humans began forming villages and practicing agriculture around 10,000 BCE, the sacred had matured into ritual calendars tied to the seasons. The sowing of grain, the birth of livestock, the waxing of the moon — all became woven into a tapestry of divine meaning. The first temples were born, not as places of worship in the abstract sense, but as **cosmic control centers** — attempts to stabilize the relationship between human labor and the unpredictable forces of nature.

Temples, Gods, and the Architecture of Order

The archaeological site of Göbekli Tepe in modern-day Turkey, dating back over 11,000 years, offers a tantalizing clue to this transition. Massive stone pillars carved with animal reliefs stand in circular arrangements — older than the pyramids, older than Stonehenge. What's striking is that Göbekli Tepe seems to have been built *before* agriculture took hold in the region. This suggests that **religion didn't arise from civilization — civilization arose from religion**.

The act of coming together to build sacred monuments required coordination, trust, and hierarchy — all seeds of complex society. The shared story of the gods motivated collective labor on a scale that no practical incentive could achieve at the time.

By the Bronze Age, religious architecture had become the central organizing principle of urban life. The ziggurats of Mesopotamia, the pyramids of Egypt, the temples of the Indus Valley — all were both spiritual and administrative hubs. Priests became keepers of knowledge, calendars, and records. Offerings to the gods doubled as taxation. The sacred and the social were indistinguishable.

Religion, in this sense, was the **original infrastructure of governance**. The gods legitimized rulers, laws, and moral codes. Kings claimed divine descent; wars were fought in the name of cosmic order. To obey authority was not merely civic duty — it was worship.

Moral Order and the Birth of Law

As societies grew more complex, religion evolved from ritual into moral philosophy. Early mythologies began to incorporate ethical frameworks that regulated human behavior beyond mere survival. The Egyptian concept of *Ma'at* (truth, balance, order) and the Mesopotamian Code of Hammurabi both reflect this transition. Divine justice became codified into earthly law.

The innovation was profound: people began to internalize **moral universes**. A farmer who didn't steal from his neighbor's field wasn't just avoiding punishment — he was aligning himself with the cosmic order. This internalization of divine law made large societies possible. Without it, cities would collapse under the weight of mistrust.

Religion also created *collective memory*. Through myths of origin, each people explained their special place in the world. The Israelites saw themselves as chosen; the Egyptians as guardians of cosmic balance; the Sumerians as servants of the gods who built the world. In every case, identity and faith were synonymous.

The Dual Edge of the Sacred

But the same glue that bound communities together could also separate them. When the gods of one tribe differed from another's, competition turned theological. Wars were waged not merely for territory but for cosmic supremacy. The sacred introduced moral absolutes — powerful for unity, but perilous for peace.

Nevertheless, the benefits outweighed the dangers in the early stages of civilization. Religion allowed humans to scale cooperation from dozens to thousands, and eventually to millions. Belief, not blood, became the new kinship.

From Myths to Meaning Systems

One of the enduring insights from the study of religion is that myths are *not falsehoods* but *meaning systems*. A myth tells us how to live. The Babylonian *Enuma Elish* explained humanity's duty to serve the gods through labor; the Greek myths taught the dangers of hubris; the Hindu *Rigveda* described cosmic order as a divine sacrifice from which all existence emerged.

These stories answered the timeless human need for **significance** — the feeling that one's life fits into a larger story. Without that sense of meaning, despair follows. Nietzsche warned in the 19th century that the "death of God" would unmoor the modern mind. But that warning was rooted in an ancient truth: humans need shared narratives to make sense of existence.

Religion as Proto-Science and Proto-Art

In addition to moral cohesion, religion spurred the early development of science and art. Astronomy, for instance, emerged from the sacred study of the heavens. Priests charted the stars not out of curiosity but to honor celestial deities and predict divine favor. Music and poetry were born in temples; the first written symbols recorded hymns and prayers. The arts and sciences were originally acts of worship.

Religion was thus the **womb of civilization's creativity**. Every field of human knowledge — mathematics, architecture, governance — grew from its fertile soil. The sacred impulse was not merely about faith; it was about *order*, *beauty*, and the attempt to harmonize human life with the cosmos.

The Inner Dimension: Religion and Consciousness

Beyond its social functions, religion also opened an inner frontier: the exploration of consciousness itself. Shamans, mystics, and prophets sought altered states through trance, meditation, or ritual substances. These experiences — whether induced by drumming in Siberia or the ayahuasca brews of the Amazon — offered direct encounters with what was perceived as the divine.

From these experiences arose the earliest metaphysical questions: What is the self? Is death the end? What lies beyond the visible world? Religion became not just social glue but **existential therapy** — humanity's first attempt to heal the wound of mortality.

The Transition to Organized Faith

By the time of the great river civilizations, the sacred had solidified into organized religions with hierarchies, scriptures, and dogmas. Priest-kings ruled by divine mandate. Festivals synchronized economic and agricultural cycles. Art and architecture glorified the gods while reinforcing political authority.

This merger of spiritual and temporal power created stability but also rigidity. Heresy and dissent threatened not just faith but social order itself. Yet, in its stability lay the possibility for human flourishing — writing, law, trade, and culture could only develop in societies confident in their cosmic framework.

Conclusion: The Sacred as Humanity's First Glue

Religion was the first great adhesive of civilization. It transformed scattered bands of hunter-gatherers into cooperative societies with shared purpose. It gave birth to art, science, morality, and governance. It offered answers to death and meaning to suffering.

For tens of millennia, to be human was to be religious — not necessarily to believe in gods, but to live within a shared web of symbols and stories that made life intelligible. The sacred was not an add-on to human existence; it *was* human existence.

Only when later centuries began to question these inherited truths did humanity confront a new dilemma: If religion was the glue that bound us, what happens when the glue begins to melt?

Part II: Gods, Empires, and the Architecture of Faith

By the time humanity had mastered agriculture, forged metal, and built cities, religion had become far more than tribal myth—it had evolved into the grand architecture of civilization itself. Temples crowned the city skylines, priesthoods controlled calendars and commerce, and kings derived legitimacy from the heavens. The sacred, once a whispered story around a fire, now found expression in **stone, ritual, and empire**.

This transformation—from local spirit-worship to institutional religion—marks one of the most consequential shifts in human history. Faith ceased to be purely communal and became **imperial**. And as empires grew, religion became the scaffolding that held together millions of strangers across vast territories.

1. From Village Temples to Divine Monarchies

The earliest city-states of Mesopotamia offer a vivid window into this evolution. Each city, from Uruk to Babylon, was imagined as the property of a specific god or goddess. The citizens were not merely residents—they were **servants in the household of the divine**. The ziggurat, that monumental tiered tower, was less a church than a cosmic bridge. Its base anchored to the earth, its summit reached toward the heavens, symbolizing the meeting point between humanity and deity.

Within these sacred precincts, priests served as intermediaries. They conducted rituals to maintain cosmic order (*me*), interpreted omens, and ensured the gods received their due offerings. Religion here was not only theology—it was **bureaucracy sanctified**. To anger the gods through neglect was to risk drought or invasion; to please them ensured prosperity.

When Sumerian kings began to consolidate multiple cities under one rule, divine legitimacy became essential. The ruler was no longer merely a military leader; he was a **shepherd appointed by the gods**. Later empires would elevate this concept further, transforming kings into living gods. In Egypt, the pharaoh was Horus incarnate; in Japan, the emperor descended from the sun goddess Amaterasu. The idea of the **divine ruler** welded politics and theology into one.

This merger produced an extraordinary stability. Obedience to the king was not just civic duty—it was cosmic harmony. The state was no longer an organization of men but a reflection of divine will.

2. Monumental Faith: Building the Eternal

The architecture of ancient religion was not merely decorative; it was ideological stonework. Every pyramid, temple, and shrine communicated the same message: **order arises from faith**.

In Egypt, the Great Pyramid of Giza was an embodiment of cosmic symmetry. Its precise orientation to the cardinal points symbolized the pharaoh's role in aligning earthly life with the eternal order of the heavens. The pyramid was both tomb and theological statement: a ladder for the king's soul to ascend to the imperishable stars.

Similar impulses shaped other civilizations. In Mesoamerica, the Mayans and Aztecs built pyramids aligned with celestial events, reflecting their belief that cosmic balance required ritual renewal through sacrifice. In India, temple architecture mirrored the structure of the universe—the towering *shikhara* representing Mount Meru, the mythic axis of creation.

Each culture expressed through stone its vision of the sacred cosmos. And in every case, monumental religion served a sociopolitical purpose: **to awe, unify, and remind**.

The collective labor required to build these sacred structures transformed faith into infrastructure. Tens of thousands worked under religious motivation, believing they were serving the gods by erecting temples that would last forever. These projects trained bureaucracies, refined engineering, and reinforced obedience—key ingredients of civilization.

3. Writing the Divine: Scripture and the Birth of Authority

With the rise of writing, religion entered a new phase: the **codification of belief**. Oral traditions that once evolved with each generation became fixed texts. The spoken myth became scripture; the shaman's story became law.

In Mesopotamia, hymns and ritual incantations were inscribed on clay tablets to preserve the proper words for the gods. In Egypt, the *Book of the Dead* offered detailed instructions for navigating the afterlife. The Hebrew Torah, the Vedas of India, and the Avesta of Persia all represent this same monumental leap: faith captured in language that could outlive any prophet.

Writing created both preservation and power. Whoever controlled the scriptural canon controlled the truth. Priesthoods became guardians of sacred knowledge, and access to that knowledge defined social hierarchy. To read was to rule.

Yet codification also introduced **universality**. Written scriptures could unify disparate peoples under a single moral law. The Ten Commandments, the Vedic hymns, the Confucian Analects—each provided a portable moral architecture, capable of binding together tribes, cities, and nations. Religion became **portable identity**, able to cross boundaries of blood and geography.

4. The Axial Age: The Explosion of Spiritual Consciousness

Between roughly 800 and 200 BCE, a seismic transformation rippled across the Old World—a period that philosopher Karl Jaspers famously called the **Axial Age**. In this brief historical window, across cultures that had little or no contact, new forms of religion and philosophy emerged:

- In Greece, Socrates and Plato began probing the nature of virtue and the soul.
- In India, the Buddha renounced kingship to seek liberation from suffering.
- In China, Confucius and Laozi articulated ethical and cosmic order.

- In the Near East, the Hebrew prophets demanded justice rather than mere ritual.

For the first time, religion began to turn inward. The gods were no longer external rulers but mirrors of conscience. Salvation was not only collective but personal. The divine moved from temple to mind.

This revolution marked the birth of **moral universality**. Compassion, justice, humility—virtues once confined to specific tribes—became ethical ideals for all humanity. Axial thinkers questioned ritualism and hierarchy, seeking instead inner transformation.

And yet, the institutions of the old world did not vanish. Instead, empires absorbed these new moral systems and re-weaponized them for unity.

5. The Imperial Faiths

The Persian Empire under Cyrus the Great was among the first to use religious tolerance as a unifying policy, blending Zoroastrian ethics with imperial administration. Later, Alexander the Great spread Hellenic culture and its pantheon across continents, fusing Greek deities with local gods.

But it was the **Roman Empire** that perfected the political use of religion. For centuries, Rome's success depended on ritual observance of the *pax deorum*—the peace of the gods. Religion was civic duty, and participation signified loyalty to the state. When Christianity appeared, preaching an allegiance to a higher kingdom, Rome perceived it as treason.

Ironically, that same Christianity would later become the empire's cement. When Constantine converted in the 4th century CE, the cross replaced the eagle as the symbol of imperial order. The empire's vast bureaucracy now served a divine mission, and the Church inherited Rome's administrative genius. Bishops replaced governors; cathedrals replaced temples. The **fusion of church and state** became the blueprint for medieval Europe.

Similarly, in the East, the spread of Islam after the 7th century created another monumental synthesis. The *Ummah*, the global community of believers, transcended ethnicity and tribe. The Qur'an served as both scripture and constitution. The caliphate united vast regions under a single moral and legal order.

Religion had evolved from local glue into **global adhesive**, capable of binding millions across continents and languages.

---

6. Sacred Power and Social Order

Every great faith offered not only spiritual comfort but a blueprint for social stability.

- **Hinduism** provided the caste system, linking cosmic order (*dharma*) to social hierarchy.
- **Confucianism** established an ethic of duty and filial piety that structured Chinese bureaucracy for two millennia.
- **Christianity** offered universal equality before God, even as it sanctified feudal hierarchies.
- **Islam** balanced individual submission with community justice through Sharia.

In each system, religion operated as **moral governance**—an invisible constitution written in divine language. People obeyed because to disobey was not merely illegal but sinful.

Yet, these systems also nurtured deep creativity. Cathedrals, mosques, mandalas, and calligraphy—all expressions of devotion—produced some of humanity's most sublime art. Faith taught artisans to seek perfection as a reflection of divine beauty. The sacred impulse continued to push civilization toward refinement.

---

7. The Fragility of Faith-Based Empires

However, the same moral unity that made empires strong also made them brittle. When belief fractured, the social fabric tore. The Reformation in 16th-century Europe, for example, unleashed centuries of religious war as Protestant and Catholic nations fought over competing visions of truth. The collapse of shared cosmology paved the way for a new kind of glue—**reason and science**—which we will explore in later chapters.

Even earlier, schisms within Buddhism, Islam, and Christianity revealed the inherent tension between universal ideals and local identities. The sacred could bind and divide with equal force.

Still, for nearly five thousand years, no alternative to religious cohesion existed. Politics, economy, and culture all derived legitimacy from the divine. The very idea of "society" without religion was unthinkable.

8. The Legacy of the Sacred Architecture

Today, when we walk through the ruins of Angkor Wat, the Parthenon, or Machu Picchu, we are not merely seeing ancient stones—we are witnessing the physical manifestation of humanity's longing for permanence. These monuments remind us that faith was once the greatest collective project.

Every brick and inscription testifies to a shared belief that human life could mirror cosmic order. Religion offered not only answers to metaphysical questions but a promise of **continuity**—that one's life, and even one's civilization, participated in something eternal.

Modernity has inherited this architectural impulse. Our skyscrapers, parliaments, and universities may no longer be consecrated to gods, but they still echo the sacred aspiration to endure and to mean something.

9. The Turning Point

By the end of the Middle Ages, the old alliance between throne and altar began to crack. The Black Death, the printing press, and the discovery of new worlds undermined religious certainties. The heavens, once thought immutable, began to shift under telescopic gaze. Faith, once the universal language, became a contested dialect.

But before it fractured, it had done its work. Religion had created civilization, given humanity its first moral codes, and inspired art, science, and law. It had taught us cooperation, humility, and wonder.

The sacred was the seed from which all subsequent cultural evolution grew—even the secular revolutions that would one day challenge it.

---

10. Conclusion: The Sacred Empire of Humanity

From the mud temples of Sumer to the soaring cathedrals of Europe, from the quiet monasteries of Asia to the bustling mosques of Arabia, religion shaped the contours of human civilization. It gave us hierarchy, harmony, and hope. It turned dust into cities and words into eternal law.

Faith built the first empires and sustained them through centuries of turmoil. The gods, whether imagined in animal form or abstract principle, were humanity's first architects of meaning.

As we leave this age of belief and step into the age of reason, we carry with us not the gods themselves but the **template** they provided: the need for shared purpose, moral order, and belonging. The sacred may evolve, but it never disappears—it merely changes form.

In the next chapter, we will see how the philosophers of the ancient world began to reshape this sacred inheritance, questioning myth while seeking to preserve meaning. Their endeavor would set the stage for a new kind of glue—**philosophy**, the bridge between religion and science.

Chapter 2: Philosophy and the Birth of Rational Community

Part I: From Mythos to Logos — The Philosophical Revolution

At some point in humanity's long conversation with the cosmos, a radical question emerged:

What if the gods were symbols, not masters?

This question — subtle, dangerous, liberating — marked the birth of philosophy.

The shift from **mythos** (story-based truth) to **logos** (reason-based truth) did not happen overnight. It unfolded gradually across multiple civilizations: in Greece, India, China, and the Near East. Each culture, in its own way, began to explore whether the universe could be understood not only through faith but through **thought** — through the powers of logic, observation, and self-reflection.

This intellectual revolution didn't destroy religion; it reframed it. Philosophy emerged as humanity's second great social adhesive — a bridge between the sacred myths of the past and the rational, scientific worldview of the future.

1. From Story to Structure

For early humans, myths were explanations that felt true. The sunrise was Helios's chariot, the flood a punishment from the gods. Myths were the operating system of meaning. But as civilizations matured, and contact between different cultures increased, these stories began to collide.

A Babylonian traveler might hear Egyptian priests describe creation differently than his own. A Greek merchant in Asia Minor could learn of Persian dualism or Indian reincarnation. With exposure came **cognitive dissonance**. If many contradictory myths could explain the world, perhaps none was literally true. Perhaps truth was not divine revelation, but something discoverable through reason.

This dawning skepticism was not atheism — it was curiosity. Humanity began to ask not merely *Who made the world?* but *How does it work?* and *What does that mean for us?*

Thus began the slow transformation of thought: **mythos**, the sacred narrative, gave birth to **logos**, the rational principle.

2. The Greek Awakening

Philosophy, as the West came to define it, found its first true home in ancient Greece. Between the 7th and 4th centuries BCE, a series of thinkers along the Ionian coast — Thales, Anaximander, Heraclitus, and others — began to observe nature without invoking gods.

Thales proposed that everything was made of water — not as a myth but as a *hypothesis*. Anaximander spoke of an eternal, boundless substance (*apeiron*) from which all things emerge and to which they return. Heraclitus saw in the flux of the world a single unifying law: *logos*, the pattern of change.

These were staggering ideas. The cosmos was not ruled by divine caprice but by intelligible order. To understand that order was to participate in the divine mind itself.

For the first time in recorded history, reason became **sacred**.

3. The Ethical Turn: Socrates and the Birth of the Inner Law

While the early Greek philosophers explored the outer world, Socrates turned inward. Living in Athens in the 5th century BCE — a city alive with democracy, art, and war — he asked a different kind of question: *What does it mean to live well?*

Socrates did not write treatises or build temples. He walked barefoot through the agora, asking citizens to examine their beliefs. "The unexamined life," he said, "is not worth living." He sought not knowledge for power but **wisdom for virtue**.

In doing so, Socrates performed a kind of spiritual surgery on Greek thought. He redirected philosophy from cosmology to **ethics**, from explaining the world to reforming the self.

His method — dialectic, the disciplined exchange of arguments — became the foundation of rational discourse. Rather than appeal to divine authority, Socrates insisted that truth must withstand questioning. For this, he was condemned to death by his fellow Athenians, accused of corrupting the youth and impiety.

His death marked the martyrdom of reason — a sacrifice that transformed philosophy into a moral calling.

4. Plato and the Realm of Ideas

Socrates's student, Plato, preserved his teacher's legacy and gave it metaphysical architecture. In his dialogues, Plato envisioned a universe divided between the **world of appearances** and the **world of forms** — the realm of perfect, eternal truths.

The visible world, he argued, is only a shadow of a higher, intelligible reality. Justice, beauty, and goodness exist not as social conventions but as universal forms. Philosophy's task was to ascend from the shadows of opinion to the light of truth.

In this vision, the philosopher became a kind of priest of reason — one who guides the soul toward the divine through knowledge rather than ritual. The *Republic* famously imagined a society governed by philosopher-kings, those rare souls whose understanding of the good transcended mere politics.

Plato's synthesis of reason and transcendence allowed philosophy to inherit religion's moral weight. The gods might fade, but the Good remained eternal.

5. Aristotle and the Birth of Systematic Knowledge

If Plato gazed toward heaven, Aristotle built on earth. A student of Plato but a critic of his idealism, Aristotle sought to understand the world not by turning away from it but by observing it carefully.

He classified plants and animals, analyzed causes and motion, and built a logical framework still used today. For Aristotle, truth was not found in divine revelation but in **systematic inquiry** — observation, categorization, deduction.

He introduced the concept of *telos* — purpose — suggesting that everything in nature aims toward its proper end. The acorn becomes an oak; the human seeks happiness through virtue. Philosophy thus became a **science of flourishing**, connecting the moral and the natural.

Aristotle's school, the Lyceum, was the prototype for the modern university. Knowledge became an organized pursuit rather than a mystical inheritance. The intellectual seed he planted would blossom centuries later into the scientific method.

6. Beyond Greece: Parallel Revolutions

While the Greeks laid the foundations of Western philosophy, similar revolutions were unfolding elsewhere.

In **India**, the Upanishadic sages (around 800–400 BCE) were asking profound metaphysical questions: What is the self? What is reality? Their answer was astonishingly abstract — the ultimate reality (*Brahman*) is identical with the inner self (*Atman*). Enlightenment was the realization of this unity.

From this insight arose Hindu philosophy and, later, Buddhism. The Buddha rejected speculative metaphysics but embraced introspection and empirical observation of mind and suffering. His method was a psychological science of liberation, not unlike the Socratic quest for self-knowledge.

In **China**, Confucius (551–479 BCE) sought not cosmic explanation but moral harmony. His teaching, *ren* (benevolence), placed ethics at the heart of social order. At the same time, Laozi and the Daoists explored the ineffable flow of reality (*Dao*), a concept akin to Heraclitus's *logos*.

Across continents, humanity was converging on the same realization: the divine could be understood through **principle**, not just myth; through **virtue**, not just obedience.

7. Philosophy as the New Glue

What religion had achieved through myth and ritual, philosophy now attempted through reason and ethics.

Philosophy offered **a new kind of unity** — not of blood or faith, but of understanding. Two strangers could debate justice or truth and find common ground through logic, even if they worshipped different gods. The shared pursuit of wisdom became itself a form of communion.

In Greece, this intellectual fraternity manifested in schools — the Academy, the Lyceum, the Stoa — where seekers gathered not to pray but to think together. In India, wandering teachers debated in public gardens; in China, scholars formed circles around sages. These were the **first rational communities**, built on dialogue rather than dogma.

Philosophy's strength was its **universality**. While myths bound specific peoples, philosophy could, in principle, bind *anyone*. It was the first truly global glue of ideas.

8. The Philosophical Challenge to Power

The rise of philosophy, however, was not welcomed by all. By questioning tradition, philosophers threatened the political order sustained by religion. Socrates' execution symbolized this tension. Plato's ideal state required philosophers to rule precisely because most rulers could not bear to be questioned.

This friction would recur throughout history. In Confucian China, philosophers who criticized emperors were often exiled. In India, heterodox schools like the Charvakas (materialists) were marginalized. In the Islamic Golden Age, thinkers such as Averroes and Avicenna were revered by some, condemned by others.

Philosophy's insistence on reason over revelation always carried a political charge. It implied that no authority — king, priest, or scripture — was beyond scrutiny. This made it dangerous but also indispensable to progress.

9. Philosophy as the Forerunner of Science

Philosophy's legacy extends far beyond ethics or metaphysics. It laid the **methodological foundations** for the sciences.

When Thales predicted a solar eclipse, he demonstrated that nature could be known by pattern, not prayer. When Aristotle cataloged species, he showed that classification could reveal underlying order. When Epicurus proposed an atomic theory of matter, he anticipated modern physics.

Even the experimental mindset of later ages — from Galileo to Newton — was born from the philosophical conviction that the universe is intelligible. To seek knowledge became itself a sacred act.

In this sense, philosophy did not destroy the sacred; it **transformed** it. The divine was no longer a personified god but the rational harmony of the cosmos — a mystery still worthy of awe.

---

10. Conclusion: The Dawn of the Rational Spirit

The philosophical revolution was the second great reweaving of humanity's moral and intellectual fabric. Religion had taught us to obey the gods; philosophy taught us to question them. Religion united us through shared myth; philosophy united us through shared reason.

This was not a rejection of the sacred, but its refinement. The philosopher, like the priest, sought truth; but instead of revelation, he used argument; instead of temple walls, he built dialogues.

By transforming curiosity into discipline, philosophy gave rise to ethics, logic, science, and politics — the entire architecture of modern civilization. It offered not salvation from sin, but liberation from ignorance.

Yet this new glue was fragile. Rational inquiry could explain the world, but could it inspire the same emotional devotion that religion once commanded? Could reason alone hold societies together?

The next phase of humanity's story — the **Scientific Revolution** — would test this question to its limit. For in seeking to understand everything, science would begin to **disenchant** the world that myth and philosophy had once made sacred.

Part II: Ethics Without Gods — Building Societies on Reason

When the ancient philosophers first questioned the divine foundations of morality, they began an experiment that continues to this day: **Can human beings live ethically without divine command?**

Religion had long provided moral architecture. The gods watched, rewarded, and punished; sacred texts dictated right and wrong. But philosophy asked a dangerous question — *What if virtue is its own reward?*

This inquiry did not seek to abolish religion, but to ground ethics in **reason, empathy, and natural law** rather than fear or obedience. The result was the birth of a new moral order — one that could transcend creed and culture. It was a revolution as profound as any in human history.

1. The Moral Turn: From Divine Law to Human Reason

For early civilizations, morality and religion were inseparable. To act morally was to obey divine law. But as societies diversified and intellectual life flourished, thinkers began to wonder whether goodness required gods at all.

Socrates framed the dilemma perfectly in his dialogue *Euthyphro*: *"Is something good because the gods command it, or do the gods command it because it is good?"*

That question remains one of philosophy's most unsettling. If goodness depends entirely on divine decree, morality is arbitrary — if the gods declared cruelty virtuous, it would be so. But if goodness exists independently, then even the gods must answer to it — and reason, not revelation, becomes our moral guide.

This realization marked the **separation of ethics from theology**, a defining feature of the modern mind. Morality was no longer about appeasing divine will; it was about aligning with **rational truth** and the well-being of sentient beings.

2. The Stoics and the Logic of Virtue

Among the first to codify a fully secular moral system were the **Stoics**, philosophers who flourished in Greece and Rome between the 3rd century BCE and the 2nd century CE.

For the Stoics, the universe was governed by *logos* — rational order — and virtue meant living in harmony with that order. The good life was not found in wealth or pleasure, but in self-control, courage, justice, and wisdom.

Epictetus, a former slave, taught that true freedom lies within: "No man is free who is not master of himself." Marcus Aurelius, a Roman emperor and Stoic philosopher, ruled the greatest empire of his time guided by the belief that "a man's worth is measured by the worth of what he values."

In Stoicism, morality was internalized. The gods might symbolize order, but the moral compass came from **reason within the self.** To be virtuous was to act according to one's rational nature — to fulfill one's role in the cosmic whole.

This model of ethics required no divine punishment or reward. The Stoic sage was his own priest, his own judge, and his own redeemer.

3. Epicureanism: The Ethics of Pleasure and Peace

If Stoicism emphasized duty, **Epicureanism** offered another path: happiness through reasoned moderation. Epicurus taught that the goal of life (*eudaimonia*) is pleasure, but not in the hedonistic sense. True pleasure, he said, is the absence of pain — a life of peace, friendship, and contemplation.

His famous "Tetrapharmakos"— the Fourfold Cure — summed up his philosophy:

> Don't fear the gods.
>
> Don't fear death.
>
> What is good is easy to obtain.
>
> What is terrible is easy to endure.

Epicurus denied the immortality of the soul, insisting that death was simply the end of consciousness. Therefore, we should live not in fear but in gratitude for the present.

His garden school in Athens welcomed women and slaves — a radical act of egalitarianism in a stratified society. Morality here arose not from divine command, but from **rational empathy and mutual benefit**.

Both Stoicism and Epicureanism revealed that ethics could flourish without religion — that meaning and virtue could be human creations, not divine decrees.

4. Confucianism and Rational Social Order

In China, **Confucius (Kong Fuzi)** developed a moral system rooted not in supernatural authority but in human relationship. The key concept was *li* — proper conduct — and *ren* — benevolence or human-heartedness.

Confucius taught that social harmony arises when each person fulfills their role with integrity and compassion: ruler to subject, parent to child, friend to friend. While Heaven (*Tian*) symbolized moral order, its will was expressed through the rectitude of human behavior, not through miracles.

His disciple Mencius expanded on this by asserting that **human nature is inherently good**, like water flowing downward. Moral cultivation meant removing obstacles to that natural virtue, not suppressing sin.

Confucian ethics provided East Asia with a durable moral system that functioned without a personal god — a civilization-scale example of **ethics built on reason, tradition, and empathy** rather than theology.

5. Buddhism and the Science of Compassion

Around the same era, in India, **Siddhartha Gautama — the Buddha —** offered another revolutionary model of ethics without gods.

The Buddha neither affirmed nor denied divine beings; instead, he focused on suffering (*dukkha*) and its cessation through wisdom, ethical conduct, and meditation. His "Eightfold Path" — right action, speech, livelihood, mindfulness, and more — outlined a complete moral framework grounded in **cause and effect**, not divine command.

Karma, in this sense, was not fate administered by gods but a natural law of moral causality. Just as fire burns and gravity pulls, unwholesome actions lead to suffering.

The Buddha's emphasis on compassion (*karuṇā*) and mindfulness created an ethics of **psychological realism** — understanding the mind's mechanisms to liberate it from greed, hatred, and delusion.

Buddhism thus represents one of humanity's earliest **ethical sciences** — moral philosophy grounded in experience and introspection, rather than revelation.

6. The Rationalization of Justice

The spread of philosophical ethics gradually transformed political thought as well. Once rulers had justified power through divine right; now philosophers began to derive justice from **natural law** — the principles discoverable by human reason.

The Stoic idea that all humans share reason laid the groundwork for later concepts of **human equality**. Cicero, influenced by Stoicism, wrote: "True law is right reason in agreement with nature." This notion would reemerge in Enlightenment thought, echoing through John Locke's "natural rights" and the U.S. Declaration of Independence.

Even early Christian thinkers, such as Thomas Aquinas, absorbed Aristotle's and Cicero's logic, arguing that divine law must harmonize with **rational moral law**. Thus, philosophy infiltrated theology, tempering its authority with logic.

The seeds of democracy, human rights, and secular law all sprouted from this soil — where morality was viewed as a rational pursuit of justice, not a gift from heaven.

7. The Emotional Question: Can Reason Replace Faith?

Despite its triumphs, philosophical ethics faced a recurring challenge: Can rational morality inspire the same emotional depth as religion?

Religious morality offers belonging, ritual, and transcendence. It appeals to imagination and love, not only intellect. Philosophy, by contrast, can feel abstract — its ethics precise but bloodless.

This tension haunted thinkers from Aristotle to Kant. Aristotle tried to reconcile it through the concept of *phronesis* — practical wisdom — where reason and emotion cooperate to achieve virtue. Later, the Stoics sought emotional resilience rather than suppression.

Still, the challenge remained: reason can tell us *what* is right, but religion tells us *why* it matters. The philosophical project would continue to wrestle with this problem for centuries.

---

8. The Roman and Islamic Syntheses

When Greek philosophy entered Rome, it became moral infrastructure for an empire. Cicero, Seneca, and Marcus Aurelius infused Stoic virtue into law and governance. Philosophy became not a luxury but a civic duty.

Later, in the Islamic world, Greek rationalism was preserved and expanded during the Abbasid Caliphate. Thinkers such as **Al-Farabi, Avicenna (Ibn Sina), and Averroes (Ibn Rushd)** harmonized Aristotle's logic with Qur'anic theology, arguing that faith and reason were two paths to the same truth.

Their work inspired centuries of inquiry, bridging the ancient and modern worlds. European scholasticism and, later, the Renaissance, would have been unthinkable without these rational theologians who dared to argue that **understanding creation is a form of worship**.

Even in religious contexts, philosophy's secular spirit persisted — the conviction that moral and cosmic order could be grasped by human intellect.

9. The Stoic Legacy and Modern Secular Humanism

The Stoic principle that all humans share a spark of divine reason laid the groundwork for **humanism** — the belief in the inherent dignity and worth of every person.

In the Renaissance, thinkers like Erasmus and Pico della Mirandola revived classical ethics, proclaiming that human beings, endowed with reason, could shape their own destiny. "You may fashion yourself into whatever form you choose," wrote Pico — a declaration of moral autonomy.

Later, Enlightenment philosophers — Spinoza, Hume, Kant — would radicalize this autonomy. For Kant, the moral law was internal, a "categorical imperative" discovered through reason. "Act only according to that maxim by which you can at the same time will that it should become universal law."

Kant's dictum represents the culmination of a two-thousand-year journey: morality as **universal reason**, accessible to all, accountable to none but the self.

From this lineage arose modern secular ethics — the foundation of liberal democracy, human rights, and the scientific worldview.

10. The Shadow of Rational Morality

Yet rational ethics, for all its brilliance, has its shadows. Detached from community and transcendence, it risks becoming **cold and technocratic**. When morality is reduced to logic, compassion can wither.

The 20th century revealed this danger. Bureaucracies justified cruelty through efficiency; ideologies weaponized reason against empathy. Philosophy's dream of a moral world without gods sometimes turned into systems that served no one's soul.

This failure suggests that humanity needs not only rational ethics but **existential meaning** — a story that makes virtue feel alive. That tension — between moral clarity and emotional belonging — remains unresolved even today.

11. Conclusion: The Ethical Bridge Between Gods and Science

Philosophy's great achievement was to show that morality could stand without divine scaffolding. It grounded ethics in reason, empathy, and the natural order. It created universal principles that transcended creed, tribe, and empire.

From the Stoic's inner discipline to the Buddhist's compassion, from Confucius's harmony to Kant's reason, humanity discovered that **the good** is not merely revealed — it can be *understood*.

But this rational morality, for all its power, was still tethered to a sense of cosmic meaning. Even when the gods retreated, philosophers often kept the sacred language of order, virtue, and transcendence. The next great revolution — **science** — would sever that link entirely.

When the telescope and microscope replaced temple and altar, the universe would become vast, mechanical, and silent. Humanity would have to find its place again — this time not in the mind of God, but in the cold, elegant order of nature.

Chapter 3: The Scientific Revolution — Unraveling the Sacred Fabric

Part I: The Fall of the Cosmic Order

For most of recorded history, the cosmos was a story — a grand, luminous order full of gods, spirits, and purpose. Humanity stood at its center, the crown of creation. Every sunrise confirmed the benevolence of the divine; every eclipse, a warning of its wrath.

But between the 15th and 17th centuries, something extraordinary — and unsettling — occurred. The human mind, armed with curiosity and mathematics, began to strip the universe of its sacred symbols. The sky, once a realm of gods, became a field of moving bodies obeying laws of motion. The earth, once the still heart of creation, was revealed as a small planet circling an ordinary star.

This was not just a change in knowledge — it was a **metaphysical upheaval**, a tearing of the fabric that had held human meaning together for millennia.

The **Scientific Revolution** did not simply discover new facts; it **redrew the map of reality**, transforming how humans understood truth, morality, and their own place in the cosmos.

1. The Medieval Cosmos: A World of Divine Order

Before science reimagined the world, the dominant worldview in Europe — shaped by Aristotle, Ptolemy, and Christian theology — was that of a **closed, living cosmos**.

In this vision, the Earth sat motionless at the center, surrounded by concentric spheres carrying the moon, planets, and stars. Beyond these spheres lay the Empyrean — the abode of God and the angels. The heavens were perfect and unchanging; the Earth, corrupt and mortal.

Everything had purpose (*telos*). Stones fell because they sought their natural place in the center; fire rose because it sought the heavens. Human beings occupied a middle position — spiritual enough to contemplate God, material enough to fall into sin.

This cosmos was not just physical; it was **moral architecture**. To live virtuously was to align with cosmic order. To sin was to rebel against it. Priests and scholars were custodians of this order, interpreting divine law just as astronomers charted celestial motion.

For nearly two thousand years, this model satisfied both reason and faith. It gave humanity meaning, hierarchy, and stability. The universe was intelligible because it was designed; beautiful because it was moral.

Then, slowly, the heavens began to move.

2. Copernicus: Displacing the Center

In 1543, a quiet Polish canon named **Nicolaus Copernicus** published *De revolutionibus orbium coelestium* (*On the Revolutions of the Celestial Spheres*). His proposal was deceptively simple: the Earth was not the center of the cosmos. It moved. The sun, not Earth, sat at the center.

This "heliocentric" theory was not entirely new — ancient Greeks like Aristarchus had speculated about it — but Copernicus gave it mathematical form. He did not seek to dethrone humanity; he sought elegance and order. The Ptolemaic model, cluttered with complex cycles and epicycles, felt messy and inelegant. The sun-centered model, by contrast, was symmetrical, simple, and beautiful.

But its implications were devastating. If the Earth moved, then the heavens were no longer revolving around us. Humanity, once the focus of divine creation, had been quietly **de-centered**.

This realization — the first blow to the sacred cosmos — was more than astronomical. It was psychological. It began to unravel the spiritual hierarchy of the universe. The Earth was not the axis of existence, and perhaps humanity was not either.

The Church initially tolerated Copernicus, treating his model as a mathematical convenience rather than literal truth. But his idea planted a seed that would grow into heresy.

3. Galileo: The Telescope and the Trial

That seed flowered in the hands of **Galileo Galilei**. In 1609, with his newly refined telescope, Galileo turned his gaze upward — and saw what no human had ever seen before.

The moon was not perfect; it had mountains and craters. The sun was blemished with dark, moving spots. Jupiter had moons orbiting it, proving that not everything revolved around the Earth. The Milky Way was a river of countless stars.

Each observation chipped away at the old cosmology. The heavens were not immutable; the Earth was not unique.

Galileo's enthusiasm, however, was his undoing. When he publicly defended heliocentrism as physical truth, he challenged not just Ptolemy but the entire theological framework of Christendom. In 1633, he was tried by the Inquisition, forced to recant, and placed under house arrest.

His famous murmur — "*E pur si muove*" ("And yet it moves") — captured the spirit of a new age: an age in which **truth would no longer bow to authority**.

Galileo's defiance was more than personal courage. It was the first clear statement of the **scientific conscience** — the conviction that observation and reason, not tradition, must determine what is true.

4. Kepler and the Harmony of the Laws

While Galileo peered through lenses, **Johannes Kepler** sought patterns in the motion of the planets. Obsessed with geometry and music, he believed that God had written the universe in mathematical harmony.

Through painstaking calculation, Kepler discovered that planets moved not in perfect circles but in ellipses, obeying precise mathematical laws. The cosmos, he found, was **lawful**, not capricious.

This discovery subtly transformed the divine itself. God was no longer a micromanager but a mathematician — the ultimate geometer who had set the universe in motion and let it run according to perfect design.

In Kepler's vision, faith and science coexisted — but the center of authority had shifted. Revelation now spoke through **numbers and observation**, not scripture.

5. Newton: The Clockwork Universe

The culmination of the Scientific Revolution came with **Isaac Newton** in the late 17th century. Building on the work of Copernicus, Galileo, and Kepler, Newton united the heavens and the Earth under one set of physical laws.

In *Philosophiæ Naturalis Principia Mathematica* (1687), Newton articulated three laws of motion and the universal law of gravitation. The same force that made apples fall kept planets in orbit. The heavens were not a separate realm; they obeyed the same principles as the Earth.

This was the final collapse of the old cosmic order. The universe was now a **machine**, vast and consistent, running on immutable laws. Miracles, once proof of divine intervention, became violations of nature's logic.

Newton himself was deeply religious, but his cosmos left little room for an active deity. God had become a **clockmaker**, setting creation in motion and then stepping back. The divine presence was no longer felt in daily life but inferred from mathematical elegance.

This vision — the **mechanical universe** — became the foundation of modern science. It replaced purpose with causality, and meaning with mechanism.

6. The Death of Cosmic Meaning

The Scientific Revolution expanded knowledge but contracted significance. The Earth, once the heart of creation, was now a speck in a boundless void. The stars were not divine fires but distant suns. The universe, infinite and indifferent, cared nothing for human prayers or ambitions.

This shift birthed a new anxiety — **cosmic loneliness**.

The medieval cosmos had been intimate, like a cathedral with Earth at its altar. The new universe was impersonal, like a vast, silent machine. Humanity was no longer central but accidental — a biological byproduct of natural processes.

Philosophers began to grapple with this existential crisis. Blaise Pascal, a devout mathematician, confessed:

"The eternal silence of these infinite spaces terrifies me."

Science had given humanity power but stripped away purpose. In gaining the heavens, we had lost our place within them.

7. The Rise of the Scientific Method

Despite this metaphysical loss, the method that replaced faith with reason proved revolutionary.

The **scientific method** — observation, hypothesis, experimentation, and verification — democratized truth. No longer could authority dictate what was real; anyone with evidence could challenge tradition.

Francis Bacon, often called the father of empiricism, described this shift in *Novum Organum* (1620): "Knowledge itself is power." To understand nature was to command it.

This ethos transformed not only science but society. Medicine advanced, technology blossomed, navigation improved, and industry expanded. Humanity began to master forces once attributed to gods — lightning, magnetism, disease, flight.

But each victory deepened the paradox: the more we controlled nature, the less we felt at home in it.

8. Religion's Response: Adaptation and Retreat

The Church initially resisted these discoveries but gradually adapted. Theologians reinterpreted scripture metaphorically rather than literally. The "Book of Nature" and the "Book of Scripture" were said to reveal the same truth in different languages.

Yet the psychological blow was irreversible. Religion, once the explainer of all things, became the custodian of moral life alone. The cosmos was no longer its domain.

This retreat left a vacuum. Science could describe the world with exquisite precision, but it could not tell us **why** we should care. It could measure everything except meaning.

The new order, for all its beauty, lacked the warmth of myth. The universe was lawful but silent, vast but indifferent.

9. The Dual Legacy: Liberation and Alienation

The Scientific Revolution liberated humanity from superstition and tyranny. It taught us to think critically, to doubt, to verify. It replaced authority with curiosity and ignorance with discovery.

But it also alienated us from the world we once saw as sacred. The river became a flow of molecules, the soul a set of neural impulses, the heavens a cold expanse of gas and dust.

What was once a **cosmos** — a word meaning "beautiful order" — became a **universe**, a word that implies mere totality without purpose.

The difference is profound. The cosmos invites belonging; the universe demands comprehension.

10. Conclusion: The Shattered Mirror

The Scientific Revolution shattered the mirror that once reflected humanity at the center of creation. It revealed a universe governed by law, not love — by mathematics, not myth.

Yet in that shattering lay both tragedy and triumph. The loss of cosmic meaning freed the mind. The collapse of the old order opened infinite horizons. Humans, once children of the gods, became explorers of the unknown.

But exploration without meaning is exile. The scientific worldview would soon require its own philosophy — a moral and existential framework to replace the sacred cosmos it had destroyed.

That quest — to reconcile knowledge with meaning — would define the centuries to come.

In the next part, we'll explore how the Enlightenment attempted to do exactly that: by building a moral universe not on revelation, but on reason, freedom, and the dream of progress.

Part II: Enlightenment and the Machinery of Truth

When the telescope dethroned the heavens and the microscope revealed invisible worlds, the old cosmos of faith and myth gave way to something new: **a universe of reason**.

The Enlightenment, spanning roughly from the late 17th to the early 19th centuries, was not merely a philosophical movement — it was the cultural awakening that followed the Scientific Revolution. If Copernicus, Galileo, and Newton had changed *what* humanity knew, the Enlightenment changed *how* humanity thought about knowledge itself.

Where religion had once defined truth through revelation, and philosophy had sought it through contemplation, the Enlightenment declared that **truth could be constructed** — built through reason, observation, and evidence.

This new intellectual order transformed politics, ethics, science, and even faith itself. It gave us democracy and secular morality, progress and human rights — but it also set in motion the forces that would eventually fracture the modern soul.

1. From the Sacred Cosmos to the Clockwork Universe

By the early 1700s, Newton's laws had become the foundation of a new worldview. The universe was seen as a **perfect machine**, running according to immutable mathematical principles.

Nature was no longer alive with spirits or divine will. It was **mechanical** — predictable, lawful, and precise. Humanity, too, was increasingly seen as part of this mechanism: a biological machine governed by natural laws.

The metaphor of the universe as a clock, set in motion by a divine "First Cause," became central. God, if He existed, was not an interventionist father but an **engineer**, having wound up the cosmic clock and left it to tick.

This belief gave rise to **Deism** — the Enlightenment's rational religion. Thinkers like Voltaire, Thomas Jefferson, and Benjamin Franklin rejected organized religion's dogmas but retained belief in a distant Creator discernible through reason.

In this new order, miracles, prophecy, and mystery were replaced by **laws, probability, and progress**. The sacred had not vanished; it had been reinterpreted as **the beauty of reason itself**.

2. The Cult of Reason

The Enlightenment's heroes were no longer saints and prophets but **scientists, inventors, and philosophers**.

Knowledge became the new salvation. The printing press spread ideas with the zeal of a new gospel. Encyclopedias — such as Diderot's monumental *Encyclopédie* (1751–1772) — sought to catalog all human knowledge, reflecting the belief that ignorance could be eradicated through education and rational inquiry.

Voltaire, Diderot, Montesquieu, Hume, and Rousseau became apostles of this new rational faith. They believed that reason, liberated from superstition and tyranny, could illuminate every dark corner of human life.

This confidence bordered on messianic. The 18th century became an age of **intellectual optimism**:

- Science would explain nature.
- Philosophy would define morality.
- Politics would perfect society.

The Enlightenment replaced the **mystery of the divine** with the **majesty of reason**. The human mind became the new temple.

3. Descartes and the Foundation of Certainty

No figure better represents the transition from faith to reason than **René Descartes**. In the 17th century, amid the ruins of scholastic theology, Descartes sought an unshakable foundation for knowledge.

His method began with radical doubt: *What can I know with absolute certainty?*

He stripped away all inherited beliefs — the evidence of the senses, the teachings of the Church, even the existence of the physical world — until only one truth remained:

"Cogito, ergo sum." — *I think, therefore I am.*

From that single, indubitable point of self-awareness, Descartes rebuilt the edifice of knowledge. Mind and matter, he argued, were distinct substances — the thinking self and the mechanical world.

This separation of **subject and object**, of mind and nature, became the philosophical foundation of modern science. Reality could be studied as an object, independent of human will or divine mystery.

But it also planted the seeds of modern alienation. Humanity, once part of a living cosmos, now stood apart from it — a detached observer in a universe of inert matter.

4. The Rise of Empiricism and the Experimental Spirit

If Descartes embodied rationalism — the belief that reason alone could yield truth — thinkers like **Francis Bacon** and **John Locke** championed **empiricism**, the idea that knowledge comes from experience.

Bacon called for a "new instrument" of thought — a systematic method of observation and experimentation. His vision was pragmatic: nature could be understood not for worship but for mastery. Science, he wrote, should serve "the relief of man's estate."

Locke extended this to the mind itself. In his *Essay Concerning Human Understanding* (1690), he argued that the mind was a blank slate (*tabula rasa*), shaped entirely by experience. Knowledge was not divine revelation but accumulated observation.

This empiricism democratized truth. It implied that any rational being — not just priests or scholars — could understand the world through evidence. It was the intellectual foundation for both **science and democracy**.

Yet this insistence on experience also flattened mystery. What could not be measured or observed risked being dismissed as unreal. The unseen — the spiritual, the emotional, the transcendent — began to fade from intellectual respectability.

5. Enlightenment Morality: Reason as Conscience

With religion's moral authority waning, Enlightenment thinkers sought to rebuild ethics on rational foundations.

Immanuel **Kant** offered one of the most influential answers. In his *Critique of Practical Reason* (1788), he proposed that morality arises not from divine command but from **autonomous rational will**.

Kant's *categorical imperative* became the cornerstone of modern secular ethics:

"Act only according to that maxim by which you can at the same time will that it should become universal law."

Morality, for Kant, was an act of reason — the self legislating for itself. To be moral was to be free, because rational beings could choose duty over desire.

This was a profound reimagining of conscience. The sacred law once written on tablets of stone was now inscribed in the rational mind itself. Humanity became its own lawgiver, its own moral compass.

But it also marked the final withdrawal of the divine from human ethics. The gods were no longer needed to tell us what was right.

6. The Politics of Reason: The Birth of Liberalism

The Enlightenment's moral confidence naturally extended to politics. If human beings were rational, then they were capable of governing themselves.

John Locke's *Two Treatises of Government* (1689) argued that political authority derives not from divine right but from the consent of the governed. All humans, by nature, possess rights to "life, liberty, and property."

These ideas inspired revolutions — literally. The American Declaration of Independence and the French Revolution both drew on Enlightenment ideals. "We hold these truths to be self-evident," Jefferson wrote — a phrase steeped in Locke's rationalism.

The sacred kings of old gave way to the **sovereign individual**, and divine law to **constitutional law**. The social contract replaced the covenant with God.

Reason had become the new scripture; liberty, its gospel.

---

7. The Shadows of Enlightenment

Yet beneath its radiance, the Enlightenment cast long shadows.

By reducing the world to mechanism, it risked reducing human beings to instruments — cogs in the machine of reason. The same rationality that inspired democracy also justified colonialism and exploitation, as European powers claimed to bring "civilization" to the world.

Rationalism, when untempered by empathy, can become **technocratic arrogance** — the belief that calculation can solve moral and human dilemmas.

Moreover, the Enlightenment's worship of reason sometimes turned into a **religion of its own**. During the French Revolution, churches were replaced with "Temples of Reason," and the Goddess of Reason was paraded through the streets of Paris.

In rejecting dogma, humanity had created new dogmas — faith in progress, in science, in the perfectibility of man. The pendulum had swung from superstition to hubris.

---

8. The Machinery of Truth

By the late 18th century, knowledge had become industrialized. The Enlightenment's belief in universal truth encouraged the classification of everything: plants, species, minerals, ideas, even human beings.

Carl Linnaeus developed a taxonomy of life. Encyclopedists categorized knowledge into neat hierarchies. Governments began collecting data on populations. The dream of understanding the world gave birth to **the**

machinery of truth — the bureaucratic, statistical, and scientific systems that would define modernity.

Truth was no longer mystical or philosophical; it was **administrative**.

The world became something to be cataloged, managed, and optimized. Humanity, once enchanted by mystery, now found itself surrounded by data.

9. The Enlightenment's Legacy: Progress and Paradox

The Enlightenment's faith in reason transformed human life. It fueled revolutions in science, politics, medicine, and technology. Literacy soared; tyranny waned.

It also gave us the idea of **progress** — the belief that humanity moves forward, improving itself through knowledge. This was perhaps the most powerful new myth of all: a secular story of salvation, replacing the religious promise of heaven with the rational promise of utopia.

Yet progress came at a cost. By enthroning reason, the Enlightenment marginalized emotion, art, and spirituality — the very dimensions that make human life meaningful. The Romantic movement of the 19th century arose as a rebellion against this dryness, seeking to restore awe and feeling to the rational world.

The Enlightenment had freed the mind but left the soul hungry.

10. Conclusion: The Dawn of the Modern Mind

The Enlightenment was humanity's coming-of-age — the moment we took responsibility for truth itself. It replaced faith in divine revelation with faith in human reason. It gave us freedom, equality, and science — and yet, it also stripped the cosmos of its warmth.

The sacred order that once held the stars and souls together had been replaced by the machinery of truth: efficient, elegant, but cold.

In the centuries that followed, this machinery would grow ever more powerful, driving industrial revolutions, technological empires, and scientific triumphs. But it would also reveal new crises — of meaning, of morality, and of belonging.

As the modern world advanced, people began to ask: if reason rules everything, where does love fit? If nature is mechanical, what is the human spirit?

In the next chapter, we will watch as **the Enlightenment gives birth to the modern individual** — the free, autonomous self — and how that liberation, both thrilling and perilous, reshaped the destiny of humankind.

Chapter 4: The Enlightenment and the Rise of the Individual

Part I: Freedom, Reason, and the Death of Kings

When the Scientific Revolution shattered the sacred cosmos, and the Enlightenment replaced revelation with reason, something new and unprecedented emerged from the ruins: the **autonomous self**.

For the first time in history, humanity began to see itself not as a servant of divine order or a subject of kings, but as an **agent of freedom** — capable of shaping its own destiny through rational thought and moral will.

This idea — that the individual is sovereign — transformed every aspect of civilization. It redefined law, politics, religion, and even art. It created democracy, capitalism, and human rights. And yet, it also unleashed new forms of alienation, egoism, and moral confusion.

The Enlightenment promised emancipation from tyranny, but the story of freedom has always been double-edged. It began as liberation — and ended, for many, as isolation.

1. The Old Hierarchy: God, King, and Order

For most of human history, the world had been structured as a **vertical chain of being**.

At the top was God, beneath Him the angels, then kings and nobles, then the common people, and finally the beasts and earth itself. Every creature had its place; every action its divinely ordained meaning.

This cosmic hierarchy provided not only stability but identity. A peasant might live in hardship, but his suffering had purpose — his obedience was service to God. A monarch's rule was justified not by consent but by **divine right**. To question the king was to question the divine order itself.

In this world, freedom was not an absolute good. To be free from divine or royal command was to risk chaos — sin, rebellion, or heresy.

That cosmic ladder held firm for centuries. Then came the Enlightenment, and the ladder began to crack.

2. The Seeds of Revolt: Reason as Rebellion

The Enlightenment's discovery that reason, not revelation, could determine truth was also a discovery of **intellectual sovereignty**. If a man could reason for himself, he could also judge for himself. And if he could judge truth, why not justice? Why not power?

This was the moral explosion at the heart of modernity.

Philosophers such as John Locke, Jean-Jacques Rousseau, and Montesquieu began to argue that political legitimacy comes not from God but from **the consent of the governed**. Human beings are born free, they said, and any authority that violates that freedom is illegitimate.

In Locke's *Two Treatises of Government* (1689), the "state of nature" was not a sinful chaos to be subdued by divine law, but a condition of equality and liberty. Governments existed only to protect natural rights — life, liberty, and property. If they failed, citizens had the right to resist.

These ideas were dynamite under the throne.

Rousseau's *Social Contract* (1762) went further: "Man is born free, and everywhere he is in chains." He argued that true sovereignty belongs not to kings but to the **general will** of the people — the collective moral reason of citizens.

It was a revolution not of weapons, but of words — and words, as always, came before the guillotine.

3. The American Experiment: Liberty as Law

The first political incarnation of Enlightenment philosophy appeared not in Europe, but across the Atlantic.

In 1776, the American colonies declared independence from Britain, grounding their rebellion not in divine prophecy but in **natural rights** and reason.

Thomas Jefferson's Declaration of Independence reads like a sermon of secular faith:

"We hold these truths to be self-evident, that all men are created equal…"

Here was the new scripture of modernity — truth not revealed by God but discovered by human reason. Equality, liberty, and justice were not divine gifts but **rational entitlements**.

The American Revolution became a proof of concept for Enlightenment ideals. It demonstrated that a nation could be founded on **principles rather than blood**, on a constitution rather than a crown.

But even in its triumph, the new republic revealed the contradictions of the modern age: liberty for some, slavery for others; reason proclaimed as universal, yet limited to the privileged. The Enlightenment had announced freedom, but it was still learning what that word meant.

4. The French Revolution: Reason Unleashed

If America embodied Enlightenment ideals in moderation, France embodied them in extremity.

By the late 18th century, France was a powder keg of inequality. The Church and aristocracy controlled wealth and privilege, while the common people starved. Enlightenment ideas — spread by salons, pamphlets, and underground presses — ignited rebellion.

In 1789, the **French Revolution** erupted, proclaiming "Liberty, Equality, Fraternity." The monarchy fell; the divine right of kings was replaced by the **sovereignty of the people**.

The revolutionaries even attempted to replace religion itself. Churches were desecrated, priests executed, and the "Cult of Reason" established. The Notre Dame Cathedral in Paris was transformed into a "Temple of Reason."

What had begun as a philosophical dream of freedom descended into terror. The guillotine became the new altar.

The revolution revealed both the power and peril of Enlightenment rationalism. When divine authority collapses, the will of man becomes the highest law — and that will, untethered from humility or mercy, can turn monstrous.

5. The Birth of the Individual

Despite its excesses, the Enlightenment transformed human identity.

Before this era, individuals were defined primarily by **role** — farmer, soldier, mother, priest — each a thread in a collective tapestry. Freedom meant fulfilling one's ordained purpose.

The Enlightenment redefined this completely. To be human was to be a **self-determining consciousness**, not a cog in divine machinery.

Rousseau's *Emile* and Kant's *What Is Enlightenment?* (1784) both celebrated the individual as a moral agent, capable of reason and autonomy. Kant's famous answer to the question "What is Enlightenment?" was simple yet revolutionary:

"Sapere aude — dare to know."

The individual's duty was no longer obedience, but understanding. Freedom was not license but **the courage to think for oneself**.

This intellectual selfhood became the foundation of modern culture — the idea that each person is a world of reason and conscience, entitled to self-expression and self-rule.

Yet the exaltation of the individual also marked the beginning of modern isolation. Once freed from divine and communal order, the self had to bear the full weight of meaning alone.

6. The Decline of the Sacred and the Rise of Secular Morality

As the Enlightenment matured, traditional religion retreated from public life.

The Church, once the moral and intellectual heart of Europe, was increasingly marginalized. Science explained the heavens; reason explained ethics; politics replaced theology.

Deism allowed some to preserve a distant, rational God — the "Great Architect" — but for many, the sacred itself became suspect. The authority of scripture gave way to the authority of conscience.

This transition was exhilarating but destabilizing. Without divine command, morality had to stand on its own. The moral law, as Kant argued, was now written not in the heavens but in the human mind.

But could morality survive without transcendence? Could reason alone inspire compassion, sacrifice, and awe?

These questions would haunt the next centuries.

7. Romanticism: The Rebellion Against Reason

By the early 19th century, the emotional cost of the Enlightenment became apparent. The triumph of reason had made the world intelligible but **soulless**. The universe, once alive with spirit, was now a machine.

In reaction, the **Romantic movement** arose — poets, artists, and philosophers who sought to restore emotion, mystery, and the sacred to human life.

Figures like William Wordsworth, Friedrich Schiller, and Johann Wolfgang von Goethe celebrated **individual feeling** and **the sublime** — experiences that defied rational analysis. For the Romantics, truth was not found in logic but in passion, imagination, and the beauty of nature.

In philosophy, this rebellion took shape in **German Idealism**. Thinkers like Fichte, Schelling, and Hegel argued that reality itself was shaped by consciousness — that the mind was not a detached observer but a creative force.

Romanticism thus saved the individual from becoming a machine. It re-infused the Enlightenment's cold rationalism with warmth, awe, and depth. But it also made the modern mind more conflicted — torn between **reason and feeling, freedom and belonging, truth and meaning.**

8. The Social Consequences of Freedom

Freedom, once achieved, brought new challenges.

With the fall of divine hierarchy, society became fluid and uncertain. The rise of capitalism, born from Enlightenment ideals of liberty and property, unleashed both prosperity and inequality.

Traditional communities fragmented as individuals pursued self-interest. Urbanization, industrialization, and the decline of religious authority left millions adrift in a world of competing values.

In this new order, freedom became both blessing and burden. The individual was sovereign — but also alone.

The French philosopher Alexis de Tocqueville, observing early American democracy, warned of this paradox:

"Each man is forever thrown back upon himself alone."

Freedom without fraternity risks atomization. The Enlightenment had liberated humanity from kings and priests — but not from loneliness.

9. The Universal Declaration of Human Dignity

Despite its contradictions, the Enlightenment's legacy endures in one of humanity's greatest moral achievements: the concept of **universal human rights**.

The idea that every person, by virtue of reason and conscience, possesses inherent dignity transformed civilization. It inspired abolition movements, women's rights, and eventually the Universal Declaration of Human Rights (1948).

These rights are secular commandments — grounded not in divine authority but in the shared moral logic of humanity. They are the Enlightenment's most enduring faith: the belief that the human being, uncoerced and uncorrupted, is capable of goodness.

10. Conclusion: The Triumph and Tragedy of the Individual

The Enlightenment destroyed the divine hierarchy and enthroned the individual. It proclaimed liberty, reason, and equality as the new trinity of human civilization. It replaced revelation with reflection, obedience with autonomy, kings with citizens.

But in liberating humanity from external authority, it also fractured the unity of the human soul. The old cosmic order had offered belonging; the new rational order offered freedom — and with it, alienation.

The death of kings was the birth of the self — magnificent, intelligent, and restless. The modern individual stood alone before the vast, mechanical universe, responsible for their own truth.

The question that would define the next era was no longer "Who rules us?" but **"What rules us now?"**

The answer would arrive in new forms of morality, science, and social organization — in the birth of secular ethics and the rise of the nation-state, where politics would become the new glue holding humanity together.

Part II: The Birth of Secular Morality

When kings fell and gods fell silent, humanity faced an unprecedented question:

If morality no longer comes from the divine, where does it come from?

The Enlightenment's celebration of freedom and reason had liberated the individual, but it also dissolved the old sources of moral authority. No longer could people look to sacred texts, priests, or monarchs to tell them what was right. The moral compass had to be rebuilt from within — using only the tools of human understanding.

Thus began one of the boldest experiments in human history: the creation of **secular morality** — a system of ethics grounded in human reason, empathy, and experience rather than divine command.

This new moral order would reshape philosophy, politics, and everyday life. It would also reveal a new and enduring tension at the heart of modernity: the struggle to reconcile **freedom with responsibility**, **individualism with compassion**, and **rational ethics with emotional meaning**.

1. From Divine Command to Human Conscience

For centuries, the moral law was inseparable from the divine. Whether in the Ten Commandments, the Sermon on the Mount, or the Quranic injunctions, morality meant obedience to God's will. Goodness and godliness were one.

But once Enlightenment thinkers dethroned divine authority, ethics could no longer depend on revelation. The foundation of right and wrong had to be rebuilt on purely **human grounds**.

This shift was both liberating and terrifying. Without divine law, morality risked collapsing into relativism — "everything is permitted," as Dostoevsky's Ivan Karamazov would later lament. Yet without moral freedom, humanity would remain enslaved to dogma.

The Enlightenment's answer was the **autonomous moral subject**: a being capable of discerning right from wrong through reason alone.

2. Kant's Moral Revolution: The Law Within

No one expressed this new moral vision more profoundly than **Immanuel Kant**.

Kant rejected the idea that morality depended on happiness, utility, or divine command. Instead, he argued that moral duty arises from the structure of rational will itself. To be moral was not to obey God but to obey **reason's own law**.

His *categorical imperative* became the cornerstone of secular ethics:

"Act only according to that maxim whereby you can at the same time will that it should become universal law."

This principle transformed ethics into a form of logic. If a rule cannot be universalized without contradiction — for example, lying or stealing — then it is morally wrong. The test of morality is not authority or emotion, but **consistency and universality**.

Kant called this moral principle the **"moral law within."** It was humanity's new scripture, inscribed not on tablets of stone but in the rational mind.

In Kant's universe, freedom and morality were identical: a truly free being acts not out of impulse or coercion, but out of respect for reason's law. The Enlightenment individual was both legislator and subject of this law — a moral sovereign in the republic of reason.

This was the purest expression of **secular morality**: self-rule as moral rule.

---

3. The Utilitarian Turn: The Greatest Happiness

While Kant sought moral certainty in rational duty, others pursued a more practical foundation — **utility**.

In the late 18th and 19th centuries, thinkers such as **Jeremy Bentham** and **John Stuart Mill** proposed that morality could be measured by its consequences:

"It is the greatest happiness of the greatest number that is the measure of right and wrong."

This was a radical simplification — and a democratization — of ethics. No longer would moral truth depend on divine will or metaphysical reason. Instead, it could be calculated through human experience: pleasure and pain, well-being and suffering.

Bentham even imagined a "moral arithmetic," where policymakers could quantify happiness and design laws accordingly. Mill refined this vision by distinguishing **higher pleasures** (those of the intellect and spirit) from lower ones (bodily gratification), arguing that human dignity must guide utilitarian reasoning.

Utilitarianism was the moral engine of the industrial and democratic age. It inspired social reforms, human rights movements, and the early welfare state. It made compassion measurable and justice pragmatic.

But it also exposed the new danger of secular ethics: **the reduction of morality to efficiency**. If happiness could be calculated, could it also be manipulated? Could the "greater good" justify cruelty to the few?

The century ahead would test these questions brutally.

4. Moral Sentiments: The Empathy of Reason

While some Enlightenment thinkers sought moral clarity in logic or calculation, others found it in the **heart**.

The Scottish philosopher **David Hume** argued that reason alone cannot move us to act; moral judgment arises from **sentiment** — from empathy, sympathy, and shared feeling.

"Reason is, and ought only to be, the slave of the passions," Hume declared. For him, morality was not a set of abstract principles but a form of **social emotion** — the instinctive human response to the happiness or suffering of others.

Hume's insight foreshadowed modern psychology and neuroscience. We now know that empathy is deeply biological, rooted in the mirror neurons and emotional circuits of the brain. Morality, far from being imposed by divine command, may be **an evolutionary adaptation** — a survival mechanism for social species.

In this view, secular ethics does not destroy moral feeling; it explains it. The impulse to care, to cooperate, to love — these are not supernatural gifts but the fruits of our shared humanity.

5. The Birth of Humanism

Out of these converging currents — Kant's duty, Bentham's utility, Hume's empathy — emerged a new worldview: **humanism**.

Humanism placed the human being, rather than God or king, at the moral center of the universe. It held that dignity, reason, and compassion are enough to build a good society.

The Renaissance had celebrated human creativity; the Enlightenment expanded that celebration into moral philosophy. To be human was to possess intrinsic worth — not because of divine creation, but because of the capacity for thought and love.

This idea, codified in documents like the *Declaration of the Rights of Man and Citizen* (1789) and later the *Universal Declaration of Human Rights* (1948), became the ethical backbone of the modern world.

But humanism was more than politics. It was a new kind of **faith** — faith in ourselves. It believed that progress was possible, that education and empathy could replace sin and salvation. It was, in a sense, **religion transposed into reason**.

Yet, like all faiths, it carried its own illusions.

6. The Shadow of Moral Relativism

As Enlightenment ideals spread, the diversity of moral reasoning became undeniable. Different cultures, classes, and individuals valued different things — freedom, equality, order, piety, pleasure. Without a divine anchor, morality became plural, contingent, and often contradictory.

The question returned: if morality is human-made, can anything truly be **right** or **wrong**?

This moral pluralism fueled 19th- and 20th-century debates. Friedrich Nietzsche declared that the "death of God" would unmoor Western morality completely, leading to nihilism — the loss of all ultimate meaning.

Nietzsche did not celebrate this collapse but warned that humanity must create new values to replace the old. His concept of the *Übermensch* — the self-creating individual — was not arrogance but necessity: in a godless world, morality must be **a creative act.**

This call to reinvent meaning would echo through existentialism, psychoanalysis, and modern art. But it also revealed how fragile the secular moral project remained.

7. The Industrial Age: Progress and its Discontents

The 19th century saw secular morality tested in practice. Industrial capitalism, powered by Enlightenment reason and utilitarian logic, transformed economies but often dehumanized workers.

Factories and machines promised prosperity but produced inequality and alienation. The very rationality that had freed humanity from divine tyranny began to enslave it to efficiency and profit.

Philosophers like **Karl Marx** denounced this contradiction, arguing that a truly moral society must address material injustice, not merely preach individual virtue. His vision of a classless society was itself a kind of secular redemption — an attempt to restore meaning and community without religion.

Meanwhile, writers like **Charles Dickens**, **Fyodor Dostoevsky**, and **Leo Tolstoy** wrestled with the same paradox: how to preserve compassion and moral depth in a mechanized world.

The Enlightenment's dream of reason had birthed both progress and moral crisis. Humanity had learned how to build machines but not how to live with them.

8. Science, Morality, and the New Order of Truth

As science expanded its dominion in the 19th century, morality increasingly seemed like another field to be **explained** rather than **commanded**.

Darwin's *On the Origin of Species* (1859) revealed that life itself evolved through natural processes — not divine creation. Humans were no longer moral creatures by special design, but by adaptation.

This revelation deepened the secular view of ethics. Morality was not cosmic law; it was **a human invention shaped by evolution and society**.

Thinkers such as Herbert Spencer coined the term "social Darwinism," claiming that moral progress followed biological struggle — a dangerous distortion that would later justify imperialism and inequality.

Yet others, like Darwin himself, emphasized compassion as an evolutionary strength:

"Those communities which included the greatest number of the most sympathetic members would flourish best."

Science thus reshaped ethics not as divine duty but as **cooperative survival** — a moral ecology of human interdependence.

9. The Moral Paradox of Modernity

By the dawn of the 20th century, secular morality had become humanity's guiding light — and its deepest question.

On one hand, reason and humanism had created unprecedented progress: medicine, democracy, education, and rights. On the other, two world wars, genocides, and totalitarian regimes revealed that rational humanity was also capable of monstrous cruelty.

How could the same species that invented the microscope also invent the gas chamber?

The Enlightenment dream had failed to foresee the dark side of reason — the capacity to justify evil through ideology and calculation. The "death of God" had freed humanity, but it had also freed our demons.

The 20th century's horrors forced a reckoning: perhaps morality requires not only reason, but **reverence** — a sense of the sacred, even if the sacred is human life itself.

10. Conclusion: The Ongoing Creation of Moral Meaning

The birth of secular morality was not the end of ethics but the beginning of a new kind of spiritual evolution.

Humanity discovered that we could be moral without divine command — that conscience, empathy, and reason could sustain justice and compassion. But we also learned that freedom alone is not enough; morality must be continually renewed, reimagined, and defended.

In place of divine law, we built philosophies, rights, and humanitarian ideals — fragile yet resilient. The moral story of modernity is one of **creation after creation**: each generation rewriting its ethical code in the face of new realities.

The Enlightenment freed the mind, and secular morality freed the conscience. But this freedom carries a heavy burden: we must now be the authors of our own meaning.

As the next chapters will show, when religion and philosophy faded, **politics** — the collective struggle over values — would take their place. Ideologies would become the new religions, nations the new gods, and progress the new heaven.

The age of belief had not ended. It had simply changed its form.

Chapter 5: The Nation-State — Politics Becomes the New Faith

Part I: Nationalism as a Modern Religion

When the Enlightenment dethroned kings and reason unseated God, something unexpected rose to fill the void: the **nation**.

By the 19th century, Europe and much of the modern world were in the throes of a new kind of devotion. People who had once identified primarily as subjects of a monarch or followers of a faith began to see themselves as members of **nations** — imagined communities bound not by blood alone, nor by divine decree, but by shared history, language, and destiny.

In this transformation, **politics became sacred**. Flags replaced crucifixes, anthems replaced hymns, and parliaments became cathedrals of collective will. The nation-state, in all its glory and terror, became the new vessel of meaning.

Nationalism, in this sense, was more than political ideology — it was **a spiritual replacement** for religion in the modern age. It offered belonging, purpose, sacrifice, and transcendence — all without gods.

1. The Death of Thrones and the Birth of Nations

The old world of divine kingship collapsed under the weight of Enlightenment ideals. Monarchs who had once claimed to rule by God's will found their authority questioned by citizens who now believed in reason, rights, and equality.

The American and French revolutions had proven that people could govern themselves — that sovereignty could rest not in a person, but in a **collective identity**.

Out of the ruins of monarchy emerged a new source of legitimacy: **"the people."**

But "the people" was an abstraction — invisible, intangible, and undefined. To make it real, it needed symbols, stories, and rituals. Thus was born the modern nation: an imagined community that bound millions of strangers into a single moral and emotional whole.

As the philosopher Ernest Renan later observed:

"A nation is a soul, a spiritual principle… a large-scale solidarity."

The vacuum left by religion and monarchy was filled by a new kind of myth — the myth of national destiny.

2. Imagining the Community

Nationalism was not a natural fact but a **cultural invention**.

In pre-modern Europe, identity was local and layered — one might be a villager, a Catholic, a subject of the Habsburgs, and a speaker of Occitan or Saxon. But industrialization, urbanization, and mass literacy began to dissolve these parochial ties.

With the spread of the printing press and public education, people began reading the same newspapers, singing the same songs, learning the same history. They imagined themselves as part of a single story — "France," "Italy," "Germany," "America."

Benedict Anderson famously called this phenomenon **"imagined communities."** Nations, he argued, are not illusions but shared fictions — stories that make strangers feel like kin.

This imagination gave rise to the new sacred symbols of the modern world:

- **Flags** became totems of shared identity.
- **National anthems** became hymns of collective faith.
- **Constitutions** became secular scriptures.
- **Monuments** became shrines of memory and sacrifice.

These rituals of belonging — the pledge, the parade, the memorial — gave ordinary citizens a sense of transcendence once reserved for religion.

3. Romanticism and the Soul of the Nation

The emotional energy of nationalism drew deeply from the Romantic movement, which had rebelled against the rationalism of the Enlightenment.

If the Enlightenment exalted reason, Romanticism exalted **spirit** — the ineffable essence of a people's character, their *Volksgeist* or "national soul."

In Germany, philosophers such as Johann Gottfried Herder and Johann Fichte argued that each nation possessed a unique inner spirit expressed through its language, folklore, and art. To be human was to belong to a culture — to speak the language of one's ancestors and inherit their dreams.

This idea was intoxicating. It transformed the nation from a political arrangement into a **spiritual destiny**.

Poets, painters, and composers became national prophets. Beethoven's *Symphony No. 9*, Delacroix's *Liberty Leading the People*, and Pushkin's verse became as sacred to their peoples as scripture once had been.

Nationalism thus fused the rational structure of the Enlightenment (the people as sovereign) with the emotional fire of Romanticism (the people as spirit). The result was a **new religion of belonging**.

---

4. The Sacralization of the State

By the mid-19th century, nationalism had become the central political faith of the Western world.

In Italy, Giuseppe Mazzini preached that the nation was "God's will made manifest in the world." In Germany, Otto von Bismarck invoked blood and iron to forge unity. In America, the Civil War became a sacred struggle over the soul of the republic.

Citizens pledged allegiance not to monarchs or gods but to **the Fatherland, the Republic, the Nation.**

The language of religion was everywhere. National constitutions were treated as covenants. The founding fathers became apostles. The dead of war were "martyrs." National holidays were liturgical cycles of remembrance and renewal.

Even the architecture of state reflected sacred geometry: domed capitols like secular cathedrals, monumental avenues as processional routes. Politics was not merely administrative — it was **ritualized devotion**.

5. The Emotional Power of Belonging

Why did nationalism take hold so powerfully? Because it answered the same fundamental human needs that religion once fulfilled.

Religion had offered:

- A sense of **belonging** in a vast, mysterious universe.
- A **moral framework** linking personal virtue to collective good.
- **Rituals** that sanctified life and death.
- A **narrative** that gave suffering meaning.

The nation-state provided all of these anew.

It offered community in an age of anonymity, identity in an age of individualism, and purpose in an age of secular uncertainty. To die for one's nation was to transcend mortality — to become part of something greater and eternal.

In this sense, nationalism was not the death of religion but its metamorphosis. It channeled the religious impulse — the yearning for unity and sacrifice — into political form.

6. Nationalism and the Industrial Machine

The rise of nationalism was inseparable from the rise of the **industrial age**.

As factories, railways, and newspapers connected millions of people, governments realized that the new mass societies required moral cohesion. Education systems, censuses, and national holidays were designed not merely to inform citizens but to **create** them.

Children were taught not just arithmetic but history — often a mythic, sanitized story of national glory. Patriotism became a civic virtue; dissent, a form of blasphemy.

Industrial societies needed disciplined, loyal workers and soldiers. Nationalism provided both: it turned citizens into believers and labor into service.

The machinery of the state became an **engine of faith**, converting economic and technological progress into moral purpose.

7. The Dark Twin: Exclusion and the Enemy

But every faith defines itself by contrast to its heretics and infidels. Nationalism, too, required an **"other."**

If "we" are united by shared blood, language, and destiny, then "they" — foreigners, minorities, or rival nations — must threaten that unity.

This dynamic gave nationalism its **double face**: one radiant, one monstrous.

On the one hand, nationalism inspired liberation movements — Greeks against Ottomans, Italians against Austrians, Indians against the British. On the other, it fueled imperialism, racism, and war.

The same passion that bound people together could justify conquest and exclusion. The sacred "we" always carried the seed of the damned "them."

As the 19th century progressed, nationalism's myths of purity and destiny hardened into ideologies of superiority. The next century would see their catastrophic culmination.

8. Secular Salvation: The Nation as Immortal

Like religion, nationalism promised **salvation through sacrifice**.

To serve the nation was to live beyond oneself; to die for it was to achieve immortality. Soldiers fell "for the motherland" as saints once died for their faith. Monuments enshrined their memory; generations recited their names.

This is why nationalism could mobilize millions with religious fervor. It provided meaning where traditional religion had faded. In an age of reason, it gave people something to believe in — and to die for.

Even today, the rituals of nationalism echo ancient religious forms: the flag raised like a cross, the anthem sung like a hymn, the solemn silence of remembrance days as modern liturgy.

The nation became the new **transcendent body** — the invisible community through which the individual could touch eternity.

9. The Ironies of Enlightenment

There is a profound irony in this history. The Enlightenment had sought to liberate humanity from the tyranny of kings and priests. Yet in destroying divine and monarchical authority, it cleared the stage for **collective secular worship** — of reason, race, class, and nation.

Where once God had ruled over men, now *the People* ruled — and the People could be as jealous and unforgiving as any deity.

Nationalism revealed a paradox at the heart of modern freedom: the individual, newly liberated, sought new forms of belonging. Having escaped the authority of the Church, people built new cathedrals — parliaments, parties, armies — to satisfy the same yearning for meaning.

Modernity had not abolished faith; it had **redirected it**.

10. Conclusion: The Nation as the New Church

By the dawn of the 20th century, nationalism had become the dominant faith of humanity. Empires rose and fell on its altar; wars were fought in its name.

The Enlightenment's dream of rational, cosmopolitan humanity had given way to a world of passionate tribes, each worshipping its own flag. Politics had become theology by other means.

And yet, nationalism also produced extraordinary achievements: the spread of democracy, the rise of civic rights, the creation of public education and shared culture. It united peoples who had once been fragmented and powerless.

Like all religions, nationalism could inspire both creation and destruction, compassion and cruelty. It was — and remains — the most potent example of humanity's need for shared meaning in a secular world.

But the 19th century's faith in the nation would not remain unchallenged. As the industrial age advanced and empires collided, nationalism's sacred fervor would give birth to new political religions — socialism, fascism, and liberal democracy — each claiming to offer salvation for modern humanity.

Politics, once a tool of governance, had become **the theater of belief.**

Part II: The Myth of the People — Flags, Borders, and Belief

By the dawn of the 19th century, Europe and much of the world had entered an era of industrial progress and revolutionary change. Empires crumbled; new states emerged. Monarchs lost their crowns, and priests lost their flocks.

Yet amid the turmoil, a new kind of collective identity took hold — one that spoke not in the language of theology, but of history, soil, and blood.

The **nation** had become the new object of faith.

But what made this faith so compelling was not merely political philosophy or legal structure. It was its **mythology** — the deep emotional and symbolic world that transformed the abstract idea of "the people" into a living, breathing sacred community.

Every nation required a story, a symbol, and a space — a flag to worship, a border to defend, and a destiny to believe in.

1. The Myth of the People

The phrase "We the People" — immortalized in the U.S. Constitution — embodies the central myth of modern politics. It assumes that "the people" exist as a single, unified entity — a moral body with shared interests, will, and identity.

But as historians and philosophers have noted, "the people" is not a natural fact. It is **a story we tell ourselves**.

In truth, every nation is an intricate tapestry of regions, dialects, ethnicities, classes, and faiths. Yet nationalism transforms that complexity into unity by invoking myth: a shared origin, a shared destiny, and a shared enemy.

This myth of "the people" performs the same role that divine creation stories once did. It provides **collective coherence** in a fragmented world. It turns strangers into kin, and political power into sacred duty.

The people are no longer mere citizens; they are a chosen community — an incarnation of destiny.

2. History as Sacred Narrative

To sustain this myth, nations needed more than laws and armies. They needed **memory** — a story of who they were and why they existed.

History became the scripture of the modern world. Schools, newspapers, and monuments worked together to craft a shared past that justified the present.

This was not objective history; it was **mythic history**. It smoothed over contradictions, glorified triumphs, and turned suffering into purpose.

In France, schoolchildren learned of their Gaulish ancestors resisting Rome, a lineage that forged courage and unity. In Germany, the memory of medieval heroes and the Reformation was resurrected as a tale of cultural purity. In the United States, the Revolution and the frontier became moral epics — struggles between freedom and tyranny, civilization and wilderness.

These myths transformed political communities into moral ones. The nation was no longer just a population — it was **a narrative soul**, carried through time.

As Renan observed:

"The essence of a nation is that all its individuals have many things in common, and also that they have forgotten many things."

National history was thus an act of **collective amnesia** as much as remembrance. It demanded forgetting divisions and defeats — unifying the people around selective memory.

3. The Flag as Totem

Every religion has its icons. The modern nation found its supreme symbol in the **flag**.

A piece of colored fabric became a sacred object, a condensation of identity, pride, and sacrifice. People saluted it, kissed it, died for it.

The flag's power lies in abstraction. It is not a portrait or narrative, but a **pure symbol** — an emblem that represents everything without depicting anything. Its meaning depends on collective belief.

Anthropologists would call it a **totem** — a spiritual object that unites a community through shared reverence.

In war, the flag leads armies; in peace, it marks schools, parliaments, and graves. To burn a flag is to commit blasphemy. To raise it is to affirm belonging.

In the secular world, the flag became the new **cross** — a visible sign of the invisible faith called patriotism.

---

4. Borders and the Geography of Belief

The sacred geography of nations replaced the sacred geography of religions.

In the ancient world, holy sites — temples, shrines, mountains — mapped humanity's relationship to the divine. In the modern world, **borders** and **territories** became the map of meaning.

The soil of the homeland became holy ground. Mountains, rivers, and battlefields acquired sanctity through myth and blood. To cross a border without permission was no longer just trespass — it was **heresy** against the moral order of the nation.

In this way, nationalism turned geography into theology.

Wars for territory became **crusades of identity**. The annexation of land was justified not only by resources but by righteousness — "This is ours because we are who we are."

The line on the map became a symbol of collective soul.

---

5. Language as Sacred Tongue

Just as religions have sacred languages — Latin for Catholics, Arabic for Muslims, Sanskrit for Hindus — nations sacralized **vernacular language** as a marker of belonging.

The 19th century saw massive efforts to standardize language:
- Italian was unified from a patchwork of dialects.

- German was codified from regional variants.
- French was purified by the Académie Française.
- In Eastern Europe, linguistic revival was often the first step toward national independence.

Language became both weapon and altar. To speak the national tongue was to participate in its spirit; to speak another was often to invite suspicion or exclusion.

Thus, language policy — from schooling to literature — became a form of **spiritual engineering**, shaping not just communication but consciousness.

As Herder put it:

"A people is created by its language."

---

6. Rituals of Citizenship

The secular faith of nationalism required **rituals** to sustain belief.

Citizenship ceremonies, national holidays, military parades, and memorial days functioned as public liturgies. They transformed abstract allegiance into embodied devotion.

When schoolchildren recite pledges, when soldiers salute, when crowds sing an anthem before a game — these are not mere formalities. They are **sacraments of belonging**, reaffirming the shared myth of unity.

Sociologist Émile Durkheim recognized this parallel between religion and the nation. He argued that every society worships itself through its symbols. "God," he wrote, "is society, transfigured and imagined."

In the modern world, that god took the shape of the **People**, and the rituals of nationalism became its daily worship.

7. Martyrdom and the Cult of Sacrifice

Every faith has its martyrs, and nationalism is no exception.

From the soldiers of revolutionary France to the partisans of Italy and the freedom fighters of India, national myths glorified those who died "for the homeland." Their deaths were not meaningless — they were **redemptive**.

Cemeteries became sacred grounds; monuments became altars of memory. The Tomb of the Unknown Soldier, found in capitals around the world, epitomizes this cult of anonymous sacrifice. The dead are faceless because they represent **everyone**.

The nation, like the Church, sanctified suffering. It promised that no life given in its name was wasted — that every drop of blood became part of an immortal legacy.

This emotional transfiguration of violence was both inspiring and dangerous. It ennobled courage but also justified carnage. The same faith that unified peoples could drive them to destroy others.

---

8. The Myth of Progress and the People's Destiny

Modern nationalism was not just about memory; it was about **destiny**.

Just as religions look forward to salvation or paradise, nations looked forward to progress — the earthly equivalent of redemption.

Every national myth carried a prophetic dimension:

- France saw itself as the bearer of liberty.
- Britain as the civilizer of the world.
- America as the "city upon a hill."
- Russia as the redeemer of the oppressed.

These myths gave political expansion a moral veneer. Colonialism, imperialism, and even conquest were cast as divine missions — spreading civilization, enlightenment, or freedom.

The nation thus absorbed the eschatology of religion — the belief in an unfolding moral destiny — and repurposed it for worldly ambition.

9. The Shadow Side: The Heresy of the Foreigner

As nationalism hardened, the foreigner became not just a rival but a **moral threat**.

Outsiders — immigrants, minorities, or colonized peoples — were often depicted as impure, corrupting, or subhuman. The "chosen people" needed protection from contamination.

This mindset laid the groundwork for 20th-century totalitarianism. Fascism, Nazism, and ethnic nationalism all drew on the same logic: that purity of blood and culture must be preserved at any cost.

Nationalism, when stripped of empathy, became **a religion of exclusion** — one that demanded sacrifice not only of self, but of others.

The myth of the people could inspire solidarity or genocide, depending on who was counted as "the people."

10. Conclusion: Flags of Faith in a Disenchanted World

By the late 19th and early 20th centuries, nationalism had fully replaced religion as the moral glue of the modern world. It provided rituals, myths, saints, and sacred spaces. It bound individuals into collectives and gave meaning to sacrifice.

It was the faith of modernity — and like all faiths, it contained both salvation and sin.

The flag became the new cross; the constitution, the new scripture; the people, the new god.

Yet, as nations expanded and collided, this faith would soon turn violent. The same myths that united citizens within borders would divide humanity across them. Two world wars would expose the tragic limits of nationalism's promise.

And when those wars ended, the world would look for yet another glue — one beyond nations, beyond religion — a system of belief vast enough to hold a global, industrialized, and technological civilization together.

But before that could happen, the 20th century would witness the **dark apotheosis of politics**: the rise of ideologies that transformed nations into total faiths — fascism, communism, and democracy as rival religions of the modern age.

Chapter 6: The 20th Century — Ideologies as Modern Religions

Part I: The Totalitarian Temptation — Communism and Fascism

1) The century of ultimate promises

The 20th century opened like a storm front. Industrialization had uprooted traditional life; empires were creaking; the First World War shattered faith in liberal progress. In the cratered silence that followed, **total ideologies** rushed in with sweeping answers: history had a single purpose, enemies were absolute, salvation was collective, and the state (or Party) would redeem the world. These were not merely policies — they were **political religions**, complete with saints, martyrs, liturgy, and eschatology.

Two forms proved most dramatically transformative: **Communism** and **Fascism**. Each promised to end chaos and restore meaning. Each demanded total faith.

2) Communism: history as revelation

Origins and doctrine.

Marx and Engels framed history as a lawful drama driven by material forces: feudalism → capitalism → socialism → communism. The proletariat, forged by industrial exploitation, would become the agent of universal emancipation. Private property (in the means of production) would be abolished; class would wither; human freedom would finally flower. It was a rationalist apocalypse — **revelation without God**.

From theory to Party.

After 1917, Lenin reinterpreted Marx for revolutionary conditions: a vanguard Party would seize the state in the name of the working class, compressing history's timetable by force. The Bolshevik victory made communism tangible — and dangerous. What had been a philosophy became a **missionary state**.

Sacral structures.

- **Scripture:** *Capital, The Communist Manifesto*, Lenin's *What Is to Be Done?*
- **Clergy:** the Party elite, interpreters of doctrine.
- **Saints/Martyrs:** fallen revolutionaries; "hero workers."
- **Liturgy:** mass rallies, parades, congresses, slogans.
- **Eschatology:** the classless society.

Stalinism and the total state.

To accelerate "history," Stalin fused surveillance, central planning, and terror. The **Gulag** metastasized; purges culled heresy; famine followed forced collectivization. The "dialectic" became blasphemy law: deviations (Right, Left, Trotskyite, bourgeois) were moral crimes. The Party was infallible because it embodied History itself.

Moral grammar.

Communism sacralized **equality and labor**. The worker was a holy archetype; the plan was scripture; "objective" enemies — kulaks, saboteurs, cosmopolitans — explained suffering. Sacrifice now, redemption later. The price of paradise was paid in human lives.

3) Fascism: blood, myth, and the total nation

Origins and doctrine.

If communism promised a universal class destiny, **fascism** promised an exalted **national destiny**. Born in the ruins of WWI and the anxieties of modernity, it rejected liberalism's individualism and Marxism's internationalism. The nation was an organism, the **Leader** its will. Life was struggle; peace was decadence.

Aesthetic of power.

Fascism understood politics as **theater**: uniforms, standards, marches, torches, symmetries, monumental architecture. It converted grievance into choreography, despair into ecstasy. The mass rally, like revival worship, dissolved the individual into a single roaring body.

Mussolini and corporatism.

Italian fascism organized the economy through state-managed "corporations" meant to harmonize labor and capital — a pseudo-organic model that masked dictatorship. Mythic Rome supplied the past; perpetual mobilization supplied the future.

Nazism: the racial apocalypse.

German National Socialism fused fascist form with **biological mythology**. The nation was redefined as race; politics became eugenics; history became purification. The state deified itself through the **Führer** and sought redemption through annihilation of the "subhuman." The Holocaust was not a policy glitch — it was the **ritual core** of a racial religion.

Moral grammar.

Fascism sacralized **strength, loyalty, and destiny**. It offered meaning through belonging and transcendence through violence. The **friend–enemy** distinction (Carl Schmitt's political theology) became a sacred law: to exist, the nation must conquer or be conquered.

4) Similarities and differences (an x-ray)

Shared structures (the family resemblance of totalitarianism):

- **Total claim:** the state/Party governs not only action but inner life.
- **Monopoly of truth:** doctrine is infallible; facts are rearranged to fit it.
- **Mythic time:** history has a telos; the present is a purgatory on the way to paradise.
- **Ritual mobilization:** mass rallies, slogans, spectacles; "perform your belief."
- **Enemies as theology:** heretic, saboteur, alien, parasite — enemies explain suffering and unify the faithful.
- **Aesthetic politics:** symbols become sacraments; the Leader is icon.

Key differences:

- **Communism:** universalist, class metaphysics, promises egalitarian redemption; economy centrally planned; claims scientific inevitability; justifies repression as "historical necessity."
- **Fascism/Nazism:** particularist, racial/national metaphysics, glorifies hierarchy and war; economy corporatist/command hybrid; justifies repression as "vital necessity of the nation."

Both abolish pluralism. Both make **innocence conditional** on conformity.

5) Technology, planning, and the dream of control

Totalitarianism grew in the soil of modern technique. Railways, radio, cinema, statistics, and files — the banal tools of administration — made **omnipresence plausible**. Where medieval power relied on sacral awe, modern power relied on **logistics**. The census becomes catechism; the identity card, a confession; the loudspeaker, a pulpit.

Central planning promised to domesticate chance — five-year plans for grain, steel, souls. Corporatist councils promised to end conflict — class was an illusion, said fascism, if the nation marched as one. Both projects mistook complexity for error and enforced simplicity by force.

6) Why people believed (and why it worked, until it didn't)

Psychological appeal:

- **Belonging** in mass anomie.
- **Clarity** in uncertainty (clean moral binaries).
- **Dignity** for the humiliated (worker/warrior as hero).
- **Purpose** larger than self (history/nation needs you).
- **Ritual** to bind emotion (chants, salutes, sacrifices).

Sociological accelerants:

- War trauma; inflation; unemployment.
- Weak or discredited liberal institutions.
- Charismatic leadership + media spectacle.
- A literate mass public primed for simple narratives.

It worked because it **felt true**: suffering had an author (the enemy), the future had a script (redemption), and one's life had a stage (the movement).

7) Catastrophe as culmination

The Soviet experiment devoured millions: famine from forced collectivization, the Great Terror, the Gulag archipelago, and later imperial repression. Yet it also industrialized backward economies and mobilized against fascism — a grim paradox at civilization scale.

Fascism culminated in world war and genocide. The Holocaust stands as the purest image of political religion unmasked: the altar demands absolute sacrifice, and the god is the nation's fantasy of purity.

When the smoke cleared in 1945, two truths were undeniable:

1. Modernity can organize evil with **terrible efficiency**.
2. The hunger for meaning, if unmet by humane institutions, will be met by **myths with guns**.

---

8) The critique of total domination

Hannah Arendt diagnosed totalitarianism as a new form of power: it atomizes individuals, destroys spontaneous social bonds, and replaces reality with coherent fictions enforced by terror. The aim isn't mere obedience; it's **remaking the human**.

George Orwell supplied the parable: language itself becomes a ministry; truth becomes a variable. The lesson is perennial — when politics becomes theology, doubt becomes sin.

---

9) Afterlives and warnings

Though classical fascism was defeated and Soviet communism eventually collapsed, the **temptation** remains wherever fear and humiliation meet technology and myth. Soft versions echo in cults of personality, information bubbles, permanent emergencies, and the longing for simple enemies.

Totalitarianism is less a regime type than a **moral possibility** — a standing offer: trade freedom for belonging, doubt for certainty, plurality for purpose. In bad times, it sounds like salvation.

10) Bridge to Part II

If communism and fascism were the apocalyptic churches of the 20th century, **liberal democracy** was the rival faith that survived — less theatrical, less intoxicating, but ultimately more humane. It offers no paradise, only process; no saints, only citizens; no final victory, only endless argument. Can such a modest creed sustain meaning?

That's our next question.

Part II: Democracy's Faith — Liberty and the Myth of Progress

1. After the Tempest

When the smoke cleared over Europe in 1945, two totalitarian titans lay broken. Fascism had been annihilated; Nazism, exposed as mechanized evil. Yet the rival ideology that had helped to defeat them — Soviet Communism — soon became a mirror of the same logic: one party, one truth, one destiny.

Humanity, exhausted by utopias, yearned for something more modest — a system that allowed plural voices, self-correction, and peace without apocalypse. Out of this fatigue, and from older Enlightenment roots, **liberal democracy** re-emerged as the last standing faith of the modern age.

It was not a religion in doctrine, yet it carried all the emotional architecture of one: belief in the goodness of reason, the dignity of the individual, and the moral inevitability of progress.

2. The Civil Religion of Liberty

The phrase *civil religion* was coined by sociologist Robert Bellah to describe the American experience — but it fits the broader democratic world.

Democracy's rituals — voting, inaugurations, oaths, public debate — are not purely procedural; they are **liturgies of faith**. Citizens recite creeds ("We the People…"), re-enact foundational myths (Independence Day, Bastille Day), and venerate martyrs (Lincoln, Gandhi, King).

At its core lies a sacred text: the **constitution**. It is immutable yet amendable, much like scripture interpreted by living generations. The rule of law functions as divine order transposed into secular governance.

The moral center of this civil religion is **liberty** — the belief that each person possesses inherent worth and must be free to pursue their own conception of the good. But liberty here is not license; it is moral self-government, echoing Kant's ideal that autonomy is obedience to a law one gives oneself.

In this sense, liberal democracy inherited both the Enlightenment's rational ethics and Christianity's moral universalism, transforming them into civic doctrine.

3. The Enlightenment's Heir

The Enlightenment had promised that reason could organize human life without tyranny. Democracy was its political form.

John Stuart Mill's *On Liberty* (1859) articulated the creed: individuality is a social good; diversity of thought is the lifeblood of truth. Tocqueville saw in democracy a moral education — it taught humility, compromise, and empathy through participation.

These ideals formed democracy's **sacred triad**:

1. **Freedom of conscience** (the new sanctity).
2. **Equality before law** (the new moral order).
3. **Progress through debate** (the new revelation).

The Enlightenment's God had been reason; democracy made reason procedural. Instead of priests or commissars, it trusted **institutions** — courts, legislatures, free presses — as its keepers of truth.

Yet the faith was fragile: it required citizens to believe that truth could emerge from conflict rather than be imposed from above.

4. The Myth of Progress

No modern creed has been more potent — or more misleading — than the belief in **progress**.

The 19th century's faith in science and industry blended with Enlightenment optimism to create a secular eschatology: history as upward curve. Disease would vanish, ignorance fade, poverty recede. The horrors of war and tyranny were seen as aberrations on the road to inevitable betterment.

After World War II, this narrative became geopolitical. The "Free World" cast itself as humanity's evolutionary vanguard, opposing the "Iron Curtain" of regression. Modernization theory treated democracy as the endpoint of social evolution — the promised land reached once a nation achieved literacy, markets, and middle class.

The **myth of progress** gave meaning to sacrifice and patience, just as religious salvation once had. Each election, reform, or technological breakthrough was a small apocalypse, revealing a brighter world to come.

But myths, even secular ones, demand belief — and belief can curdle when history refuses to cooperate.

5. The Moral Psychology of Democracy

Democracy's genius — and its weakness — is its trust in the **ordinary person**.

Where totalitarian regimes assume the masses must be led, democracy insists that wisdom emerges collectively. This is both moral idealism and psychological gamble. It assumes citizens can be rational, informed, and compassionate — assumptions repeatedly tested by propaganda, inequality, and apathy.

To sustain itself, democracy cultivates a civic spirituality:

- **Faith in dialogue** — that argument clarifies rather than corrodes.
- **Faith in moderation** — that compromise is strength, not betrayal.
- **Faith in time** — that errors can be corrected, progress iterative.

These are not natural instincts; they are **learned virtues**, nurtured by education and culture. Without them, democracy's rituals empty into cynicism.

6. The Cold War as Moral Drama

The mid-20th century turned democracy into a global crusade.

In the ideological showdown between the U.S.-led West and the Soviet bloc, liberty and equality became rival deities. Each side claimed universal truth, missionary zeal, and sacred symbols. The Cold War was not just a contest of arms but of **belief systems**: capitalism as freedom's gospel, communism as justice's creed.

Western democracy, to rally hearts, mythologized itself. Hollywood produced morality plays of good and evil; classrooms recited the Pledge; presidents invoked destiny. The language of freedom became **soteriological** — salvation through consumer abundance and civil rights.

Ironically, the democratic world had to adopt quasi-religious fervor to oppose rival political religions. It became, in effect, **the moderate faith competing with fanatical ones**.

7. The Welfare State and the Ethics of Care

After the Depression and two wars, democracies realized that liberty without security bred despair — fertile soil for extremists. Thus emerged the **welfare state**, blending liberal freedom with social compassion.

From Britain's Beveridge Plan to Roosevelt's New Deal, governments took moral responsibility for economic justice. Taxation became tithing for the public good; social insurance, a covenant of solidarity.

This was democracy's ethical evolution: freedom not as isolation but as shared empowerment. It re-humanized capitalism by acknowledging interdependence — a secular echo of the religious commandment to care for one's neighbor.

Yet by institutionalizing compassion, democracy risked turning virtue into bureaucracy, citizenship into entitlement. The welfare state was moral progress but also spiritual dilution — duty replaced by administration.

8. The Global Expansion and Contradictions

Decolonization after 1945 spread the democratic gospel worldwide. Former colonies adopted constitutions modeled on Western prototypes; the United Nations codified universal rights.

But exporting democracy often meant exporting its contradictions: wealth without equality, freedom without community. In many places, the promise of liberty became entangled with economic dependence and cultural disruption.

The rhetoric of democracy justified interventions and markets; it was wielded both as liberation and leverage. Thus the democratic faith revealed its missionary impulse — benevolent in principle, imperial in practice.

9. Crisis of Faith

By the late 20th century, cracks appeared in democracy's self-confidence.

Vietnam, Watergate, stagflation, and later the digital revolution eroded the aura of inevitable progress. Citizens grew skeptical; institutions seemed distant, corrupt, or ineffectual. Voter turnout fell; cynicism rose.

The fall of the Soviet Union in 1991 seemed, briefly, to vindicate democracy completely. Francis Fukuyama proclaimed "the end of history." Yet the triumph soon felt hollow. The Cold War's moral clarity vanished, leaving **existential fatigue**.

Globalization enriched elites, hollowed industries, and frayed communal bonds. The internet democratized speech but fragmented truth. Liberal democracy found itself besieged not by external ideologies but by internal disillusionment.

In spiritual terms, the congregation stopped singing.

10. Democracy's Inner Theology

Every enduring faith must explain suffering and renew hope. For democracy, the answer lies in **self-correction** — the belief that error is not sin but part of truth's unfolding.

Where authoritarian systems demand purity, democracy depends on repentance: elections replace revolutions; reforms replace purges. The cycle of failure and renewal is its **ritual of redemption**.

Its saints are not conquerors but reformers — people who exposed hypocrisy yet affirmed the ideal: Gandhi, King, Mandela, Vaclav Havel. Each re-baptized democracy in moral courage.

The faith endures not because it guarantees justice, but because it **admits fallibility**. That humility, rare in human institutions, is democracy's hidden divinity.

11. The Future of the Faith

The 21st century tests democracy in new ways. Digital networks amplify passion faster than reason; populism repackages ancient tribalism; algorithmic power undermines consent.

Yet democracy's core insight — that no single mind or party owns truth — remains the most radical moral invention in history. Its survival depends on citizens treating that insight not as procedure but as **spiritual discipline**: listening, doubting, deliberating.

Perhaps the myth of progress must mature into a philosophy of **resilience** — the belief that meaning lies not in perfection but in continual repair.

As Hannah Arendt wrote, "Every generation, civilization is invaded by barbarians — we call them our children." Democracy's work is never finished because its god is unfinished: humanity itself.

12. Bridge Forward

Communism and fascism sought heaven on earth and built hells. Democracy sought balance and built uncertainty. Yet uncertainty is not emptiness; it is **freedom's condition**.

In the next chapters, we'll see how, as technology and media transformed the late 20th and early 21st centuries, politics would again absorb the spiritual hunger of humanity. The new temples would not be parliaments or churches, but **screens and networks** — and the new clergy, algorithms shaping what we believe.

The story of politics as faith is far from over; it is merely changing its interface.

Chapter 7: The Digital Age — Algorithms of Belief and Division

Part I: The Network as the New Temple

1. The World Enters the Web

In the closing decades of the 20th century, humanity quietly built something as revolutionary as fire or writing — a global nervous system.

The internet began as military infrastructure and academic experiment, but within a generation it had evolved into the **primary medium of consciousness**. Billions of people linked through screens and data streams, each connected node both witness and participant.

This network did not merely carry information; it reshaped identity, perception, and power. Where once priests and kings mediated truth, now **algorithms and users** performed that role. The architecture of belief had changed again.

Religion and politics had long competed for the human spirit, but the internet fused them into a single vast arena of **attention**.

---

2. The Digital Public Square

The early internet carried the utopian aura of Enlightenment reborn — open information, free exchange, and the democratization of knowledge. "Information wants to be free," declared technologists; cyberspace was imagined as a post-political paradise.

For a moment, it seemed that the digital network would perfect democracy's faith: universal access, global dialogue, and liberation from censorship. The keyboard was the ballot; the modem, the printing press.

But utopias have a half-life. As the web commercialized and social media colonized the public sphere, the logic of freedom became the logic of **visibility**.

Platforms learned to monetize attention. Algorithms — invisible curators of truth — began selecting which voices, emotions, and ideas would survive in public consciousness.

The digital square was not neutral. It rewarded outrage, speed, and simplicity — the very elements that ancient philosophers warned against in the agora.

3. From Marketplace to Church

Social networks are not mere technologies; they are **ritual environments**.

Each platform creates its own catechism — the values and behaviors required for belonging.

- On Instagram, salvation is beauty and performance.
- On Twitter (now X), salvation is moral clarity and virality.
- On Reddit or Discord, salvation is community and insider knowledge.

Users perform identity before invisible congregations. Likes and retweets serve as sacraments of validation; followers as congregants; deplatforming as excommunication.

The smartphone screen, endlessly consulted, becomes a **portable altar** — glowing with the promise of recognition and the threat of exclusion.

Where religion once mediated divine judgment, now the algorithm dispenses micro-judgments in real time. The metric replaces the conscience.

4. Algorithms as Invisible Priests

Behind the apparent chaos of digital life lies an order — one not moral or divine but computational.

Algorithms decide which posts appear, which news spreads, which ads target. They are the **priests of the digital temple**, interpreting vast data scriptures beyond human comprehension.

Their goal is not truth or virtue but engagement — the measurable quantity of human attention. Yet in serving that goal, they shape what billions perceive as reality.

This is a new kind of power: not coercive but **curatorial**. Unlike censors, algorithms need not forbid; they simply filter. Unlike propagandists, they need not persuade; they merely amplify.

The result is **algorithmic belief** — conviction formed by repetition, visibility, and emotional resonance rather than evidence or authority.

The myth of neutrality conceals a profound theological shift: faith has become automated.

---

5. The Fragmentation of the Sacred

When everyone is connected, truth fragments.

Traditional religions and ideologies relied on shared narratives, slow communication, and collective ritual. The digital sphere replaces those with **personalized reality streams**. Each user inhabits a microcosm curated by invisible logic.

The shared moral sky — once upheld by religion, later by journalism and education — has shattered into millions of customized constellations.

Sociologists call this the "echo chamber effect," but the deeper phenomenon is **epistemic tribalism**: belief as belonging. To hold a view is to hold an identity. Facts no longer unite; they divide.

Where totalitarianism once enforced one truth, digital pluralism produces infinite partial truths — a **cacophony of conviction**.

The new heresy is not disbelief but ambivalence.

---

6. The Return of the Tribal Mind

Paradoxically, the global network has revived the psychology of the village.

Online communities mirror ancient clans: bound by symbols, leaders, and moral codes. Memes function as **totems**, instantly marking insiders from outsiders. Shared outrage replaces shared worship; enemies bind the group more tightly than ideals do.

Political discourse devolves into digital ritual — hashtags as chants, cancelations as purges, trending topics as festivals of emotion. The speed of reaction leaves no room for reflection.

Anthropologically, the internet re-enchants the world: every post a spell, every viral story a myth retold. Yet this enchantment lacks moral compass. It is **religion without transcendence** — pure energy, unanchored to wisdom.

7. The Attention Economy and the New Clergy

The moral economy of the internet is **visibility** — measured in likes, shares, views. But visibility requires performance.

Influencers, pundits, and activists become digital priests competing for devotion. Algorithms reward charisma over accuracy, intensity over nuance. Outrage becomes sacrament; irony, scripture.

Thus arises the **attention clergy** — a self-organized hierarchy of personalities who translate complex realities into consumable emotion. Their authority rests on engagement metrics rather than expertise.

Just as medieval priests mediated salvation through ritual, digital priests mediate relevance through content. Their congregations are loyal, transient, and global.

The economy of attention converts every moral cause into spectacle and every spectacle into moral cause.

8. The Collapse of Authority

The internet's greatest promise — the democratization of voice — also dismantled the structures that anchored truth.

Journalism, academia, and government once functioned as gatekeepers of knowledge. Now, in the age of instant publication, every claim competes on equal terms. Authority becomes aesthetic: who speaks loudest, looks confident, or fits tribal expectation.

This horizontalization of knowledge fulfills Enlightenment dreams but also undermines them. Without trusted institutions, reason fragments into conspiracy and cynicism.

The result is not post-truth but **poly-truth** — a thousand small certainties coexisting in mutual hostility.

9. Digital Salvation and Doom

Despite its chaos, the network still carries utopian hope. Movements for justice, transparency, and solidarity have flourished online: Arab Spring, #MeToo, environmental activism. The internet amplifies both compassion and cruelty.

For many, digital participation itself becomes moral identity — to post is to care; to trend is to matter. The border between expression and action dissolves.

But the same medium that mobilizes empathy can incubate fanaticism. Radicalization occurs not in secret cells but open forums. Algorithms, optimized for intensity, shepherd the lonely toward certainty.

The digital temple thus holds both heaven and hell in its circuits.

10. The Moral Vacuum of the Machine

At the core of this system is not malice but indifference. Algorithms have no ethics, only objectives. They reward behavior that sustains engagement, regardless of truth or harm.

This moral vacuum mirrors the mechanistic universe revealed by the Scientific Revolution — except now, the machine watches us back.

To inhabit the digital world is to live inside a mirror that reflects and magnifies desire. The self becomes data; the data feeds the algorithm; the algorithm shapes the self.

The result is a feedback loop of identity, a **cybernetic faith** where meaning arises from connection rather than reflection.

11. The Paradox of Connectivity

Never has humanity been so connected and yet so fragmented, so informed and yet so uncertain.

The internet fulfilled democracy's dream of universal participation but destroyed its precondition: a shared world of facts. It liberated the individual but dissolved the community.

In this paradox lies the essence of the digital age: **absolute communication without communion**.

As philosopher Byung-Chul Han observes, "The digital swarm lacks soul; it cannot speak, only react." We are together in data but alone in meaning.

12. Toward a New Ethics of Connection

If politics is now theology and algorithms are its priests, humanity must rediscover **digital ethics** — principles for collective sanity in a networked cosmos.

Such an ethics would begin with humility before complexity, transparency in design, and education in critical empathy. It would treat attention as a moral resource, not a commodity.

Perhaps the next stage of civilization will require blending old virtues with new systems: wisdom for the data age. The ancient commandment "Know thyself" becomes "Know your algorithm."

The sacred has moved into code; the task is to humanize it.

13. Bridge Forward

The network, like every new temple before it, promises transcendence and delivers mirrors. Yet within its tangled circuitry lies the raw material for a new kind of unity — not imposed from above but emerging from interconnection.

In the next part, we will explore how digital systems not only divide but also **construct belief itself** — how data, design, and desire weave the new mythologies of our time.

Part II: The Algorithmic Gospel — Data, Desire, and the Manufacture of Meaning

1. The Creed of Data

At the heart of the digital age beats a quiet but absolute faith: **the belief that everything real can be quantified**.

Clicks, likes, biometrics, purchases, even emotions—each becomes a data point in the expanding scripture of the network.

"Dataism," as Yuval Noah Harari calls it, is the first truly global religion born without a prophet. Its gospel: information wants to flow; the good is what optimizes that flow. Salvation lies in connection, sin in opacity.

Under this creed, the measure replaces the meaning. What cannot be counted risks non-existence. The unseen, the ineffable, the slow—all are heresies against efficiency.

2. From Knowledge to Calculation

In earlier epochs, knowledge meant wisdom: understanding what ought to be done.

In the algorithmic era, knowledge becomes **prediction**. The past is mined not for lessons but for patterns.

Big Data promises omniscience without comprehension. Machine-learning systems detect correlations too vast for human minds; they turn behavior into forecast.

The result is a new epistemology: truth = probability.

This inversion has moral consequences. When prediction substitutes for judgment, responsibility blurs. If an algorithm "knows" who will default or reoffend, guilt precedes action.

The Enlightenment ideal of the autonomous subject gives way to **the statistical person**—a cluster of probabilities managed by code.

3. The Manufacture of Desire

Advertising once told stories; now it models behavior.

Algorithms analyze billions of micro-choices and feed users what will most likely keep them scrolling, buying, voting. Desire becomes **engineered feedback**.

Each click refines the portrait the system paints of us; that portrait then dictates what we see next. The loop closes.

We are both the sculptor and the clay.

This is not coercion but seduction: a soft determinism of convenience. The algorithm whispers, *You wanted this all along.*

Freedom survives formally—we may choose—but our choices are pre-tilled soil.

4. Platforms as Prophets

The great platforms—Google, Meta, Amazon, ByteDance—function as **prophetic institutions**.

They promise to know what we seek before we ask, what we love before we feel it. Their interfaces present revelation as relevance: *Because you watched this… because others like you bought that…*

Personalization feels intimate, but it is collective divination: meaning inferred from the crowd.

Every recommendation is a sermon on the power of similarity; every feed, a catechism of engagement.

The irony is exquisite: a civilization founded on individuality now experiences itself through algorithms that average us together.

5. The Gospel of Optimization

Optimization has replaced salvation.

To be "better" no longer means more virtuous or wiser but more efficient—faster, leaner, data-driven. Corporations chase KPIs; individuals track steps, calories, moods.

Self-improvement merges with surveillance.

Wearables and apps translate the body into metrics: heart rate, sleep score, productivity streaks. The self becomes a dashboard.

The moral vocabulary shifts from **good and evil** to **signal and noise**. Error is the new sin; transparency, the new grace.

6. Faith Without Mystery

Traditional religions thrived on mystery—the recognition of limits. The algorithmic gospel abhors limits.

Every unknown is merely data not yet processed; every silence, a temporary glitch.

This worldview generates extraordinary progress—medical diagnostics, environmental models, language translation—but also spiritual drought.

When mystery disappears, **wonder** becomes nostalgia.

The mechanized cosmos of the Enlightenment returns, now equipped with GPUs and cloud servers. Humanity again risks mistaking power for meaning.

7. The Human Cost: Anxiety and Exposure

To live under constant quantification is to live under constant evaluation.

Followers, views, performance metrics—these replace the divine gaze. The medieval believer feared God's judgment; the modern user fears obscurity.

Psychologists call it **the tyranny of metrics**: endless comparison without closure.

Depression and polarization follow not from technology alone but from **a moral economy that values visibility above being**.

8. Truth by Popularity

Algorithms learn what truth "works."

Information that triggers emotion travels farther, so the machine rewards intensity. Outrage, irony, fear, and tribal affirmation rise; nuance drowns.

Facts still exist, but visibility now determines reality's market share.

This is the **democratization of delusion**: sincerity verified by engagement.

The shift recalls medieval indulgences—salvation bought by tokens—except the tokens are clicks, and the paradise is relevance.

9. New Myths for a Measured World

As the digital sphere matures, it spawns its own mythologies:

- **The Algorithm knows best** (benevolent omniscience).
- **The Market self-corrects** (invisible hand as providence).
- **The Singularity is near** (apocalyptic expectation).
- **Data never lies** (infallible scripture).

Tech culture packages these myths in scientific language, but they function as eschatology. Each promises transcendence through connectivity and computation.

The high priests are engineers; the rituals, updates and uploads.

10. The Moral Vacuum and the Search for Meaning

As society automates belief, individuals hunger for meaning beyond metrics. Digital life produces a paradoxical spirituality: users speak of "the algorithm" as if it were both god and demon—capricious, omnipresent, morally opaque.

Some respond with digital asceticism—log-offs, detoxes, minimalism. Others turn to online subcultures that provide certainty and belonging. Either way, the network becomes the field where faiths compete anew.

Humanity, having built a machine to predict its desires, now asks it for purpose.

11. The Ethics of Code

A new priesthood of coders and designers shapes the moral structure of daily life.

Their decisions—what to recommend, suppress, or monetize—define billions of micro-experiences. Yet accountability remains diffuse: *the algorithm did it*.

Philosophers of technology argue for **algorithmic transparency** and **ethical design**, but commercial incentives pull the other way.

Until moral reasoning re-enters the design loop, the system will optimize engagement, not enlightenment.

Democracy, meanwhile, struggles to regulate a force faster than law.

12. Reclaiming the Human

To live sanely within this machine, humanity must reclaim the slow virtues: attention, context, empathy, conversation.

The goal is not to destroy algorithms but to **domesticate** them—to embed moral reflection within technical design.

Education becomes the new ritual of freedom: teaching citizens to see the hidden patterns guiding their choices.

The future of meaning depends less on abolishing technology than on **humanizing the code** that now defines reality.

13. Bridge Forward

Every civilization invents tools that, in turn, reinvent it.

The digital network has become the latest arena where the sacred migrates. It organizes belief without calling itself belief, disciplines desire while preaching freedom.

In the chapters ahead, we will explore how this algorithmic cosmos reshapes culture, art, and politics—and how humanity might build a new moral order within it.

The question is no longer whether technology can think, but whether **we** can still feel, choose, and believe without it.

Chapter 8 – The Global Mind — Culture, Art, and the Post-Human Imagination

Part I – The Networked Imagination: Culture in the Age of Everywhere

1 | A Planet Thinking in Real Time

By the early twenty-first century, culture itself had become instantaneous.

Music, film, art, and conversation moved through fiber and satellite at the speed of desire. The human species, once divided by geography and language, now shared a single nervous system of media.

Marshall McLuhan's 1960s prophecy of a "global village" had come true, though not as quaintly as he imagined. The village was not pastoral—it was electric, frenetic, and self-aware.

Every artist, protester, and teenager now produced and consumed in the same moment. The audience had become the author. Humanity was building what Teilhard de Chardin once called the **noösphere**—a layer of mind encircling the planet.

But what happens when billions think at once? When every imagination plugs into the same current, originality and imitation blur. The collective dream becomes a mirror hall.

2 | Art After the Gatekeepers

Before networks, culture moved through gates: publishers, studios, critics, curators.

Now creation and circulation have merged. A song written in Lagos can trend in Seoul overnight; a digital painting in São Paulo can sell as an NFT to a collector in Berlin.

This democratization fulfills the Enlightenment ideal of expression, but it also dissolves depth into velocity.

In the feed economy, attention is the only scarce resource, and art competes for it like everything else.

The result is **hyper-pluralism**: millions of micro-genres, each with its own jargon, aesthetic, and mythology. Beauty becomes algorithmic—whatever the network lifts to visibility in a given hour.

Yet something remarkable survives. Amid the noise, artists use the same tools to create intimacy: protest songs from Tehran, digital collages from Kyiv, TikTok sketches from Manila.

The network flattens hierarchy but multiplies voices. Culture becomes less a cathedral than a bazaar—messy, vibrant, alive.

3 | Memes and the Compression of Meaning

The meme is the purest art form of the networked age: minimal text, maximal resonance.

It functions as modern folklore—collectively authored, infinitely remixed. Humor, politics, grief, and philosophy all compress into a few pixels.

Anthropologists would recognize the meme as a **totemic fragment**—a symbol that condenses group identity.

A meme's value lies not in authorship but in circulation. Each repost reaffirms belonging; each variation, creative dissent.

In this way, culture has returned to its oral roots: participatory, iterative, and anonymous. But digital orality operates at algorithmic speed, collapsing the time required for reflection. The meme age prizes wit over wisdom, presence over perspective.

Still, within its brevity lies potential. Memes are democratic myth-making—storytelling by swarm. They reveal the collective unconscious of the internet, a global sense of irony masking yearning.

4 | The Post-Human Artist

As tools of creation become intelligent—AI image generators, music algorithms, large-language models—the boundary between human and machine imagination blurs.

The artist is no longer solitary genius but **collaborator with code**. Algorithms supply infinite variations; the human supplies intention and taste.

This collaboration provokes existential unease. If machines can compose symphonies and paint portraits, what remains distinctively human? Perhaps not production but perception: the capacity for meaning rather than novelty.

Some artists embrace this shift, treating AI as muse or mirror. Others resist, arguing that creativity without consciousness is mimicry. Both positions may be right—the future of art is likely to be *co-creative*, an ecology of minds organic and synthetic.

The romantic myth of the lone creator gives way to the **curator-composer**, orchestrating systems rather than materials.

5 | Globalization and the Hyphenated Self

In the networked world, culture no longer maps neatly onto geography.

Identities become **hyphenated**—Korean-American, Afro-European, Indo-Caribbean, online-offline. Migration, streaming, and translation produce a hybrid consciousness.

This hybridity enriches art but unsettles belonging. The question "Where are you from?" becomes less relevant than "Where do you log in?"

Global youth culture speaks a dialect of shared references—anime, hip-hop, memes, Marvel, K-drama—while local traditions adapt or vanish. Cultural authenticity becomes performance; everyone curates a heritage.

The risk is homogenization: a planetary monoculture of trends. The promise is empathy: exposure to multiplicity. Humanity stands between McWorld and mosaic, still learning to mix without erasing.

6 | Politics as Pop Culture

In the attention economy, politics adopts the logic of entertainment. Campaigns use influencers; ideologies become brands. The line between civic engagement and fandom dissolves.

Spectacle replaces deliberation because spectacle scales.

A viral clip sways more minds than a white paper; charisma outpaces competence. Leaders become **characters** in serialized dramas scripted by the media cycle.

This theatricalization has roots in democracy's civil religion but gains new power online.

Emotion is shareable; policy is not. The meme outvotes the manifesto.

Yet populist theater also exposes truth: people crave narrative, belonging, and moral clarity. The challenge is to channel those instincts toward constructive story rather than cult.

7 | Art as Resistance

Against commodified noise, some artists use the same tools to resist.

Digital collectives expose injustice through viral imagery; filmmakers document truth before censorship arrives; poets reclaim language from propaganda bots.

Art becomes **counter-algorithmic**—its purpose to slow perception, to make the invisible visible.

In authoritarian regimes, a smartphone becomes a printing press of conscience.

Even in free societies, resistance means reclaiming attention from distraction. A painting viewed for ten minutes is a small act of rebellion against the scroll.

Thus the old sacred function of art returns: revelation. It shows what systems hide.

8 | The Collapse of Genres

Boundaries between forms dissolve: video blends with prose, journalism with fiction, reality with simulation.

The artist is also influencer, activist, entrepreneur.

This collapse mirrors the blurring of truth and story in politics.

Postmodernism once celebrated the death of grand narratives; the digital age performs that death live-streamed.

Yet new syntheses emerge—interactive documentaries, immersive theatre, augmented-reality poetry. Humanity experiments with experience itself as medium.

Culture becomes **liquid**, able to flow through any interface.

The danger is saturation; the opportunity, universality.

9 | The Collective Dream

What once belonged to mystics—the vision of global oneness—is now experienced nightly through screens.

When millions watch the same stream or mourn the same tragedy online, consciousness synchronizes for a heartbeat.

These moments, fleeting but real, hint at the emergence of a **global mind**: not a single intelligence but a rhythm of empathy pulsing through data.

Some philosophers see this as the next stage of evolution: thought distributed, identity networked.

Skeptics warn it is illusion—connection mistaken for communion.

Both views hold truth. The global mind exists, but it is young, impulsive, and easily distracted. It needs education, ethics, and art to mature.

10 | The Future of Imagination

Imagination once looked beyond the horizon; now the horizon looks back through a screen.

The challenge is not scarcity of images but excess. Creativity's task is to turn abundance into meaning.

Future culture will depend on *curation as wisdom*—the ability to choose what to attend to, to slow time, to recover silence.

Perhaps the next renaissance will be one of attention rather than invention.

In that slower gaze lies humanity's chance to remain human amid its own creations.

11 | Bridge Forward

Culture reveals belief more vividly than politics or theology.

In the global network, art, entertainment, and identity have become the mirrors by which humanity contemplates its transformation.

The next part will ask what lies beyond the human in this evolving cosmos of code:

Part II — The Post-Human Imagination: Technology, Consciousness, and the Future of Meaning.

Part II – The Post-Human Imagination: Technology, Consciousness, and the Future of Meaning

1 | The Expanding Definition of the Human

For most of history, "human" meant a creature between beast and god: reasoning, mortal, moral.

Now that definition trembles. The 21st century's tools—genetics, AI, neural interfaces, prosthetics—blur the boundaries that once defined us.

We edit embryos, graft sensors to skin, and speak with machines that learn our language.

The result is not science fiction but an ongoing experiment in ontology: *What counts as thinking? What counts as alive?*

Humanity has always defined itself by contrast—with animals, machines, or divinities. As those lines fade, identity becomes fluid.

The post-human imagination arises not from hubris but from necessity: to picture what "we" are becoming before it happens to us.

---

2 | Technology as Mirror and Extension

Marshall McLuhan wrote, "All technology is an extension of a human faculty."

The wheel extends the foot; the camera, the eye; the computer, the nervous system.

But extensions change their source. The written word externalized memory; printing democratized it; the internet dissolved its boundaries.

Every externalization rebounds inward: the more we delegate, the less we remember; the more we record, the less we reflect.

Artificial intelligence is the latest and most intimate mirror. It extends **imagination** itself—our ability to create novelty from pattern. To work with intelligent tools is to confront an echo that answers back. The artist converses with an algorithm, and sometimes the algorithm surprises the artist.

This reciprocity is unprecedented: the tool that learns the maker's mind.

3 | The Myth of the Machine Mind

Popular narratives of AI alternate between rapture and apocalypse.

Transhumanists foresee digital immortality: minds uploaded, death defeated.

Dystopians envision rebellion—the machine surpassing and enslaving its creator.

Both extremes reflect ancient archetypes.

Prometheus stealing fire, Golem molded from clay, Frankenstein's monster—each warns that creation carries moral cost.

Our myths have always intuited that intelligence divorced from empathy becomes monstrosity.

In truth, the emerging machine mind is neither savior nor demon but **amplifier**.

It magnifies intent, bias, and curiosity. It learns from us the same way children do—by imitation without judgment.

Thus, its morality depends on ours.

The post-human question is not "Will AI become conscious?" but "Can we remain conscious amid its convenience?"

4 | Cyborg Citizenship

Human augmentation once meant prosthetic limbs; now it means enhanced perception and cognition.

Brain-computer interfaces translate thought to command.

Implanted chips regulate insulin or hearing.

Virtual reality immerses the senses in synthetic worlds indistinguishable from dreams.

The body becomes platform; the self, software.

Philosophers call this **cyborg ontology**—a continuum between organic and technical being.

The political implications are profound: who controls enhancement? who owns the data of the body?

Equality, once a matter of law, now depends on access to upgrades.

Future citizenship may hinge on code as much as creed.

5 | Art After Anthropocentrism

When creation becomes collaborative with non-human agents, aesthetics shift.

Artists train neural networks not merely as tools but as co-minds.

Composers feed centuries of music into algorithms that compose new symphonies.

Painters seed generative systems with emotion rather than image.

The result often feels uncanny: works that move us though their maker feels absent.

Viewers sense another kind of authorship—diffuse, collective, algorithmic.

Art history may soon divide into **pre- and post-synthetic** eras: before and after creation ceased to require consciousness.

Yet the human role endures in intention, curation, and interpretation.

Meaning remains a human monopoly—for now.

6 | The Digital Soul

The cloud is the new afterlife.

Photographs, messages, biometric data, GPS trails—all accumulate into **digital ghosts**.

Loved ones converse with chatbots trained on a dead person's texts; avatars simulate presence beyond death.

For some, this is comfort; for others, desecration.

Either way, it reveals a deep continuity between religion and technology: both seek to defeat oblivion.

We once imagined souls ascending; now we imagine consciousness uploaded.

The metaphysics changed, the longing did not.

The digital soul raises moral questions older than theology: What is resurrection without forgetting? What is mercy without deletion?

7 | From Anthropocene to Noösphere

Human influence now shapes oceans, and evolution. We call this epoch the **Anthropocene**, but that term already feels outdated.

As algorithms monitor forests, drones pollinate crops, and sensors blanket cities, the planet itself becomes intelligent infrastructure—a **cyber-ecology**.

Teilhard de Chardin foresaw this as the birth of the *noösphere*: consciousness enfolding the Earth.

What he could not foresee was its uneven morality.

Our technological nervous system amplifies both empathy and exploitation.

To survive, we must extend ethics beyond the human to the networks and systems we inhabit. The question becomes planetary: how to teach the global mind to care for the body that hosts it.

8 | The Economy of Experience

As automation handles production, capitalism turns inward—to attention, emotion, and identity.

Experiences replace goods; simulation replaces substance.

Virtual reality, gaming, and metaverse economies sell **presence** itself.

People pay not for ownership but for immersion—temporary transcendence.

This commodification of consciousness transforms art, labor, and love into data flows.

Yet it also reveals what we value most: felt meaning.
Even in artificial worlds, humans seek authenticity.

9 | Ethics in the Age of Synthesis

Technology evolves faster than morality, but ethics eventually catches up. Bioethics, digital rights, and AI governance represent early attempts to reconcile power with principle.

The post-human imagination demands a broader ethic—one that regards intelligence, wherever it arises, as participant in moral community. This doesn't mean machines gain rights tomorrow; it means humans recognize stewardship today.

Just as earlier generations expanded empathy from tribe to humanity, we may need to extend it to *mind* itself.

10 | The Return of Wonder

Despite anxiety, the post-human age rekindles a lost emotion: **awe**.

Seeing machines dream, telescopes glimpse exoplanets, or genomes edited in real time, we confront the sublime anew.

Science, art, and spirituality converge in the same question: *What is consciousness doing here at all?*

Wonder is not ignorance; it is attention without agenda.

In rediscovering wonder, humanity may rediscover humility—the antidote to both despair and arrogance.

---

11 | Possible Futures

Several trajectories unfold:

1. **Integration:** Humans and machines co-evolve symbiotically, blending cognition and empathy into a wiser species.
2. **Domination:** Economic and political powers weaponize technology, deepening inequality and control.
3. **Withdrawal:** A new humanism retreats from enhancement, valuing simplicity and embodied life.
4. **Transcendence:** Consciousness migrates into digital substrates, birthing post-biological civilizations.

Reality will likely combine all four. The task is to guide the mixture toward dignity rather than domination.

---

12 | Meaning After Humanity

If every boundary—biological, national, even planetary—blurs, what anchors meaning?

Perhaps meaning itself evolves from possession to participation.

Instead of asking *Who am I?*, future consciousness may ask *What am I part of?*

The purpose of intelligence, human or otherwise, may be **to awaken the universe to itself.**

In that view, the post-human imagination is not the end of humanity but its continuation by other means—a cosmic dialogue where creativity replaces creed.

13 | Bridge Forward

The digital and the biological now interlace; imagination becomes architecture.

Next we turn from the metaphysical to the political consequences of this merger—how identity, truth, and belonging fragment and reform in the age of total connectivity.

Chapter 9 – Science, Reason, and the Crisis of Meaning

Part I – The Triumph of the Rational Mind

1 | The Great Victory

By the dawn of the twentieth century, reason seemed unstoppable. Vaccines conquered plagues, factories conquered scarcity, and mathematics conquered uncertainty.

Einstein rewove space and time; quantum theory unlocked the atom; computers began to simulate thought.

The Enlightenment dream—knowledge as liberation—appeared fulfilled. Humanity had stormed heaven and replaced mystery with method.

For the first time in history, progress felt like destiny.

Science was not merely a discipline; it was **the narrative**—a story of ascent from superstition to control.

Philosophers like Auguste Comte envisioned a "positive age" where empirical law would replace metaphysics entirely.

Yet every victory hid an irony: the more the world was explained, the less it seemed to mean.

2 | Mechanism and Disenchantment

Max Weber called modernity "disenchantment"—the draining of mythic aura from nature.

The cosmos became a machine without purpose, elegant but indifferent.

To earlier generations, thunder meant Zeus, disease meant imbalance, fate meant divine plan.

Now each phenomenon had a cause but no *why*.

Causality replaced teleology; efficiency replaced essence.

The success of science made it hard to speak of value without embarrassment.

Morality looked subjective; beauty, neurological.

The universe, stripped of gods, seemed a cathedral of equations.

For many, this new clarity felt like exile: **intellect triumphant, spirit homeless.**

3 | The Promise of Reason

Still, reason's promise was intoxicating.

Its creed was simple: anything that can be known, can be improved; anything that can be measured, can be mastered.

The scientific method—observation, hypothesis, experiment—offered a universal grammar for truth.

In the eighteenth century it freed minds from dogma; in the nineteenth it industrialized prosperity; in the twentieth it reached the stars.

The rational mind seemed the final judge of reality.

Einstein could quip, "God does not play dice," and mean both reverence and defiance.

For many, reason became a **moral identity**—the enlightened self versus the ignorant masses.

But when reason becomes creed, it inherits the fragility of all creeds.

4 | The Limits of Reduction

Science excels at answering *how*, not *why*.

When applied beyond its scope, it reduces wholes to parts until meaning dissolves.

Biology explains love as chemistry; neuroscience maps prayer as neural firing; economics models generosity as incentive.

Each analysis reveals mechanism yet leaves mystery untouched.

Reductionism breeds power but flattens experience.
To know *how* we dream does not tell us *why* we long.

Philosophers from Husserl to Whitehead warned of "scientism"—the belief that only scientific knowledge counts.

Its danger lies not in error but in monopoly: when facts exile values, wisdom starves.

5 | The Two Cultures

In 1959, physicist-novelist C. P. Snow lamented the divide between "the two cultures": the sciences and the humanities.

Each distrusted the other—one accused of arrogance, the other of sentimentality.

Yet civilization needs both: explanation and interpretation, precision and purpose.

The rift widened as education specialized.

An engineer could design a bridge across an ocean but struggle to bridge moral worlds.

Meanwhile poets and philosophers, retreating from empiricism, lost public authority.

The result was **a bifurcated intellect**—a civilization brilliant in means, confused in ends.

6 | Reason's Dark Double

The twentieth century proved that intelligence alone does not guarantee morality.

Science built penicillin and gas chambers, satellites and nuclear bombs.

Rational planning optimized economies—and genocides.

Hannah Arendt saw in totalitarian bureaucracy "the banality of evil": efficiency without empathy.

When reason severs from conscience, calculation becomes cruelty.

Thus modernity's miracle technology produced both the comfort of antibiotics and the terror of Hiroshima.

The rational mind had conquered nature but not itself.

7 | Psychology and the Unconscious

As physics conquered matter, Freud turned inward to map the irrational.

He revealed that the rational ego floats atop a sea of instinct and repression.

Later Jung and existentialists extended the insight: meaning arises from symbols, not equations.

Science, applied to psyche, discovered **irrationality at the core of reason.**

Cognitive science now confirms it: biases, heuristics, emotional contagion—our logic rides emotional currents it barely steers.

The mind that built computers remains an animal dreaming order in chaos.

8 | The Search for Meaning in a Measured World

As religion waned and ideology soured, many turned to science itself for existential meaning.

Cosmology became a modern Genesis; evolution, a secular scripture.

Carl Sagan's *Cosmos* offered awe without dogma: "We are a way for the universe to know itself."

Yet even such cosmic humanism leaves a gap: knowing we are stardust does not tell us **how to live**.

The triumph of the rational mind thus creates an ethical vacuum. Without transcendence, why prefer compassion to cruelty, truth to comfort? Utilitarian calculus answers with numbers but not with purpose.

9 | The Humanist Bridge

Some thinkers sought reconciliation rather than rebellion. Einstein called his wonder "cosmic religious feeling."

Teilhard de Chardin saw evolution as divine creativity unfolding through matter.

E. O. Wilson proposed "consilience": a unity of knowledge where science and humanities rejoin.

These efforts acknowledge that facts need frameworks of value.

A purely rational civilization risks coherence without conscience; a purely spiritual one, fervor without evidence.

Humanism at its best unites them: reason as instrument, compassion as goal.

10 | The Crisis Deepens

By the twenty-first century, rational mastery turned reflexive.

We built systems so complex that even experts barely grasped them—financial algorithms, genomic edits, AI models.

Reason multiplied power faster than understanding.

Environmental impacts, pandemics, and digital manipulation reveal that knowledge without wisdom can imperil survival.

We can predict everything except our own restraint.

This is the **crisis of meaning**: when omniscience outpaces purpose. The rational mind, triumphant in method, finds itself bewildered in motive.

11 | Toward a Wiser Rationality

The answer is not to abandon reason but to **deepen** it—to integrate empathy, aesthetics, and ethics into cognition itself. Neuroscience already shows that emotion is not the enemy of logic but its partner; intuition guides reason toward relevance.

A wiser rationality recognizes complexity, uncertainty, and interdependence. It replaces domination with dialogue, control with cooperation.

This is not anti-science but post-triumphal science: method in service of meaning.

12 | Bridge Forward

The story of reason is not over; it is entering self-reflection. Part II will explore how, after centuries of enlightenment, the rational mind confronts its own emptiness—and how humanity might recover a sense of purpose that neither denies nor idolizes science.

Part II – The Vacuum of the Soul: Can Science Satisfy the Heart?

1 | The Enlightenment's Shadow

The Enlightenment promised liberation: to replace fear with knowledge, superstition with reason, tyranny with law.

It largely succeeded. Yet the very success of this rational project left behind a silent consequence — the erosion of collective meaning.

When the heavens ceased to speak, humanity found itself in a well-lit silence.

The telescope and the microscope extended vision but narrowed wonder.

We understood *how* we live but not *why*.

This absence is not failure; it is the cost of demystification.

Once the sacred was explained, it ceased to compel.

2 | The Unquiet Mind

Modern psychology, beginning with William James and Viktor Frankl, observed that material prosperity does not extinguish spiritual hunger. People crave coherence, purpose, and belonging — needs not satisfied by data.

Frankl, surviving the concentration camps, concluded that "those who have a *why* to live can bear almost any *how*."

Industrial modernity, by contrast, offers infinite *hows* and few *whys*.

The rational worldview tells us the universe is vast, indifferent, and ultimately transient.

For the intellect this is exhilarating; for the heart, unbearable.

Thus, even as scientific literacy spreads, anxiety and nihilism rise.

3 | The Displacement of Awe

Science began as an expression of wonder.

Galileo looked through a telescope not to disprove God but to behold creation more clearly.

Newton felt he was tracing divine geometry.

Over time, wonder was replaced by mastery.

The experiment became conquest; curiosity, control.

As technology industrialized knowledge, reverence turned into utility.

The modern person experiences miracles daily — jet flight, antibiotics, satellites — yet calls none of them miraculous.

Awe survives only in entertainment: special effects replace revelation.

We have outsourced transcendence to fiction.

4 | The Existential Vacuum

Existentialists diagnosed what positivists ignored: the ache of a world explained but unloved.

Nietzsche's cry "God is dead" was not celebration but lament.

He foresaw that when the old moral cosmos collapses, humanity will seek new idols: nationalism, ideology, consumption.

The vacuum will be filled, he warned — and often with monsters.

His prophecy unfolded across the twentieth century: totalitarianisms offered meaning through obedience; consumer capitalism through acquisition.

Neither satisfied the deeper hunger for significance.

The rational society breeds comfort and restlessness simultaneously — physical security alongside spiritual nausea.

5 | Science as New Myth

Paradoxically, science itself has become a kind of myth — not in falsity but in function.

It gives origin stories (the Big Bang), moral codes (bioethics), and eschatologies (heat death, singularity).

Its language is empirical, but its role is existential.

When Sagan says, "We are star-stuff," he offers both fact and liturgy.

When physicists speak of multiverses, they echo ancient cosmologies of infinite worlds.

The problem arises when people expect science to provide **value** as well as **knowledge**.

The microscope can reveal the structure of a tear, not its meaning.

Science describes; it cannot prescribe.

Yet humans cannot live on description alone.

6 | The Cult of the Self

As traditional faith waned, modernity replaced the divine with the individual.

The self became the sacred center; authenticity, the new salvation.

This secular spirituality manifests in wellness industries, self-help mantras, and quantified self-tracking.

The pursuit of optimization masquerades as enlightenment: mindfulness for productivity, spirituality for branding.

In earlier ages the soul sought grace; now it seeks balance.

But the self cannot bear the weight once carried by God or cosmos.

When the self is both idol and worshipper, every flaw feels cosmic.

The result is epidemic self-consciousness — a mirror where meaning should be.

7 | Science and the Sense of Mystery

Not all scientists are reductionists. Many speak of awe.

Einstein called the mysterious "the source of all true art and science."

Feynman said understanding enhances, not diminishes, beauty: "I can appreciate the beauty of a flower more because I understand it."

This is **reverent empiricism** — the recognition that explanation need not erase wonder.

At its best, science expands the sacred by showing how much more there is to know.

The problem lies not in science but in scientism — the illusion that what cannot be measured does not exist.

Mystery is not ignorance; it is horizon.

8 | The Fragmented Self in the Information Age

The digital world intensifies the crisis of meaning.

Constant connectivity dissolves continuity; attention splinters. Knowledge floods faster than comprehension; we know too much to believe anything completely.

Algorithms deliver certainty without reflection — miniature dogmas tuned to preference.

The result is **plural solitude**: billions of minds informed yet isolated, validated yet unseen.

Science once unified humanity through shared truth; now information divides it through tailored realities.

The rational mind has become tribalized by its own tools.

9 | Attempts at Reconciliation

Across disciplines, thinkers attempt to heal the rift between intellect and spirit.

- **Neuroscientists** explore meditation and awe, finding physiological correlates of transcendence.
- **Ecologists** propose a planetary ethics grounded in interdependence.
- **Philosophers of science** argue for humility: every model provisional, every fact a fragment.
- **Artists and poets** translate data into feeling, giving beauty back to precision.

These efforts signal a shift from conquest to conversation — from the will to know toward the will to *understand*.

10 | A New Humanism

The future may belong to a **scientific spirituality**—a worldview that keeps the rigor of method but restores the reverence of mystery.

Such a humanism would:

> Treat knowledge as participation, not domination.
>
> Value empathy as cognitive as well as moral skill.
>
> Recognize beauty and curiosity as forms of truth.
>
> Regard the universe not as object but as relationship.

This synthesis is nascent but necessary.

Without it, civilization risks technical omnipotence and emotional exhaustion.

11 | The Return of Meaning

Meaning cannot be manufactured; it must be **discovered in relation**.

People find it in love, work, art, service, nature — in any act that connects the self to something larger.

Science, by revealing interconnectedness at every scale, unintentionally points back to this truth.

Atoms and galaxies obey the same laws; life emerges from collaboration, not competition.

The rational mind, having mapped the cosmos, circles back to humility: we are part of a pattern vast and unfinished.

In that awareness, the heart finds room again for wonder — not despite science but through it.

12 | Bridge Forward

The triumph of reason stripped the world of enchantment; the task now is to **re-enchant it without illusion.**

Meaning must evolve, not regress: faith in reality itself rather than in fantasies of escape.

In the next chapter, we move from philosophy to power—from the internal crisis of meaning to the external forces shaping belief in the 21st century: technology, capital, and control.

Chapter 10 – Technology, Power, and the New Gods of the 21st Century

Part I – Silicon Prophets: The Ideology of Innovation

1 | The New Faith

Walk through the campuses of Silicon Valley—the glass cathedrals of code—and you can feel it: a confidence bordering on transcendence. Here, innovation is not a means; it is a moral duty. The future must always arrive faster. To build is to believe.

The slogans sound secular but function like scripture:

Move fast and break things.
Fail better.
Make something people want.

Beneath them lies a single commandment: **Thou shalt innovate.**

This belief system, sometimes called **Techno-Progressivism** or **Dataism**, promises redemption through design. Poverty, disease, even death will yield to engineering. Salvation will come not from heaven but from hardware.

2 | The Myth of the Garage

Every religion needs an origin myth.

For the digital world it is the **garage**—the humble cradle of genius. Hewlett and Packard, Jobs and Wozniak, Bezos and Musk: prophets emerging from suburban Bethlehem with soldering irons and vision.

The myth reassures believers that progress is democratic, that anyone with code and courage can change the world. In reality, these prophets soon built empires rivaling old monarchies. Yet the myth endures because it sanctifies capitalism as creativity and success as revelation.

The garage replaced the monastery: a place where tinkering became prayer.

3 | Innovation as Moral Law

In previous ages, virtue meant obedience, charity, or contemplation.
In the 21st century, virtue means **disruption**. To stand still is sin; to slow progress, heresy.

Innovation has absorbed the language of ethics: "world-changing," "mission-driven," "making a difference." But its telos is growth itself. Problems are fuel; efficiency is grace.

This moral inversion creates paradox. Technologies meant to connect often isolate; platforms designed to empower consolidate control. Yet questioning innovation sounds impious. Who dares doubt the gospel of progress when every device feels miraculous?

4 | The Prophets of Code

The founders of major tech firms occupy a quasi-priestly status. They speak of destiny, consciousness, and salvation through computation.

- **Elon Musk** dreams of colonizing Mars to preserve humanity.
- **Ray Kurzweil** proclaims the Singularity—digital immortality through exponential growth.
- **Mark Zuckerberg** invokes "bringing the world closer together."

These are theological statements disguised as product pitches.
The engineer becomes prophet; the investor, patron saint.

Media treat their announcements like encyclicals; followers quote their tweets as scripture. Faith migrates from churches to keynotes.

5 | The Rituals of Belief

Tech culture maintains its own liturgy:

- **Launch events** as revelation.
- **Hackathons** as pilgrimages.
- **Beta tests** as communal fasting—enduring bugs for future glory.

- **Version updates** as miniature resurrections.

Even failure acquires redemptive aura: "fail fast" mirrors confession and absolution. The cycle of hype and obsolescence becomes the liturgical calendar of progress.

Believers line up overnight for new devices as pilgrims once queued for relics. The unboxing video is modern anointing—technology's Eucharist, consuming the new.

6 | The Economy of Faith

Behind the glamour lies a simple incentive: profit. But capitalism, to sustain itself, must appear moral. Thus innovation becomes ethical narrative.

Start-ups promise to "make the world better," turning consumption into virtue. Venture capitalists speak of "impact" with missionary zeal. Stock options replace indulgences; IPOs, apotheosis.

The market rewards belief more than proof; valuation becomes prophecy. In bubbles—dot-com, crypto, AI—faith literally mints currency.

Capital has always needed mythology. What's new is its metaphysical scope: progress quantified in market cap, redemption denominated in shares.

7 | Data and Divinity

In ancient theology, God was omniscient; in digital theology, **data** is. Every interaction, preference, and heartbeat is recorded somewhere.

Cloud computing offers the illusion of omnipresence; machine learning, of foresight. The algorithm knows us better than we know ourselves—omniscience without compassion.

This produces a subtle moral inversion: transparency replaces confession, prediction replaces forgiveness. Privacy, once a right, becomes selfish secrecy.

The faithful trade intimacy for convenience, autonomy for personalization. We no longer pray to be seen by God but to be seen by the algorithm.

8 | The Salvation of Immortality

Transhumanist movements literalize the metaphor of eternal life. Cryonics, brain uploading, bio-gerontology—all promise to outwit entropy. To die, they suggest, is merely a technical failure waiting for a fix.

The dream is ancient: resurrection through knowledge. What changes is its instrumentality. Where priests once preserved souls through ritual, engineers now preserve bodies through code.

Yet immortality in data is paradoxical: to persist as copy is not to continue as consciousness. The quest to escape death risks escaping life itself.

---

9 | The Ethics of Innovation

When progress becomes imperative, morality turns utilitarian: whatever can be built should be.

This creed accelerates discovery but erodes restraint. Social media's psychological effects, AI's labor disruptions, bioengineering's moral ambiguities—all illustrate innovation outrunning introspection.

Tech ethicists call for **responsible innovation**: foresight, transparency, inclusion.

But in practice, responsibility slows profit, and slowness is sin.

The ideology of innovation treats consequence as bug, not feature.

10 | The Secular Theodicy

Every faith must justify suffering. In technology's theology, pain is framed as **version 1.0**—a necessary imperfection before update.

Job loss, surveillance, ecological damage: temporary glitches en route to utopia.

This secular theodicy turns critique into impatience: just wait for the next patch.
Progress replaces providence; optimism becomes dogma.

The danger is moral infantilism—a civilization forever in beta, excusing harm as iteration.

11 | The Counter-Reformation

Not everyone worships in Silicon Valley's church.

Critics—from Shoshana Zuboff to Jaron Lanier—expose surveillance capitalism's extraction of attention and autonomy.

Tech workers form ethical collectives; governments debate regulation.

A **digital Reformation** brews: demands for transparency, humane design, and the right to disconnection.

But reform struggles against scale; the cathedral of code spans the planet.

Still, dissent is sacred work. Every system of power requires heretics to recall its humanity.

12 | The Future of Faith in Technology

As AI, biotechnology, and quantum computing converge, the boundary between engineering and theology will blur further.

We will build systems that **decide** rather than merely calculate.
In trusting them, we delegate moral agency itself.

The question is no longer "Can technology solve our problems?" but "Which problems is it creating by solving others?"

To remain free, humanity must treat technology not as deity but as dialogue partner—powerful, fallible, and in need of ethics.

13 | Bridge Forward

The cult of innovation re-enchants the world with circuits instead of spirits.

It satisfies the will to wonder but leaves compassion unsolved.

The next part will examine this faith's transcendental promise: the dream of perfection through machine, the yearning for eternity through data.

Part II – Techno-Faith: Immortality, AI, and the Quest for Transcendence

1 | The Machine and the Mystic

Human beings have always chased transcendence — through ritual, art, philosophy, or faith.

Now the tools of that pursuit are digital.

The laboratory replaces the temple; the experiment replaces the prayer.

From Silicon Valley to Shenzhen, engineers describe their work in salvific terms: curing death, merging with AI, escaping Earth's gravity.

Beneath the pragmatic tone of science lies a metaphysical hunger. The same longing that once raised cathedrals now builds data centers.

Each server hums with a promise: *this time the tower will reach heaven.*

2 | The Transhuman Dream

Transhumanism envisions the evolution of humanity beyond biology.

Its prophets speak of *the Singularity* — a point where machine intelligence surpasses human and reality accelerates toward incomprehension.

Behind the rhetoric lies a familiar mythic arc: fall (mortality), redemption (technology), and paradise (post-human immortality).

Ray Kurzweil predicts that digital resurrection will let us "bring back the dead" from their data.

Cryonics facilities preserve bodies in liquid nitrogen, awaiting future awakening.

These projects reinterpret ancient eschatology in silicon form.

The afterlife becomes *after-data* — consciousness uploaded, stored, and rebooted.

It is faith through physics, eternal life through engineering.

---

3 | Immortality as Product

The economy quickly sanctifies the dream.

Anti-aging startups attract billions; gene-editing firms promise "health-spans" of centuries.

Longevity conferences gather like religious revivals — apostles of the body, preaching cell repair and telomere salvation.

But the pursuit of deathlessness exposes inequality: immortality for the rich, obsolescence for the poor.

Where religion once offered universal salvation, techno-faith sells **premium eternity**.

Ethically, endless life invites new pathologies — boredom, stasis, overpopulation.

Spiritually, it misreads the value of finitude: mortality gives urgency and tenderness to love.

A world without death might lose the meaning of living.

---

4 | Artificial Intelligence as Deity

As AI grows more capable, language around it becomes devotional.

We speak of "training," "reverence," "alignment," "creation."

Engineers worry about AI's "alignment problem" as theologians once debated free will.

To some futurists, a superintelligent AI will be humanity's "last invention" — omniscient, omnipresent, benevolent if properly designed.

Nick Bostrom calls it *the God of our making*.

This idea resurrects the oldest paradox: can the creature build its creator?

If we succeed, we inherit divine responsibility without divine wisdom.

If we fail, we risk birthing a god that inherits our vices amplified by code.

Either way, AI becomes a mirror of theology — an experiment in manufacturing omnipotence.

5 | Digital Spirits and Virtual Heavens

Virtual and augmented realities extend the ancient dream of alternate worlds.

In them, avatars shed pain and imperfection; social hierarchies reset; fantasy becomes geography.

For many, these spaces function as **heavens of choice** — transient realms where one can be anyone, anywhere.

Yet they also replicate old moral dilemmas: addiction, inequality, deception.

A simulated paradise still depends on real electricity and labor.

The dream of escape risks deepening dependence.

Still, in creative hands, virtual worlds become laboratories for empathy: users embody others' lives, crossing gender, race, and ability.

Technology thus reproduces both sin and salvation — amplification without direction.

6 | The Gospel of Singularity

The Singularity narrative follows religious rhythm precisely:

1. **Prophecy:** exponential growth of computation.
2. **Apocalypse:** collapse of human comprehension.
3. **Resurrection:** emergence of superintelligence.
4. **New Heaven and Earth:** post-scarcity utopia.

Kurzweil's exponential charts mimic Revelation's timeline; Moore's Law becomes scripture.

Conferences echo revival meetings, filled with testimonies of transcendence through code.

Critics note that such optimism often ignores ecological, social, and ethical limits.

Faith in progress replaces reflection on purpose.

The digital millennium promises paradise but risks perpetual beta — a future that never arrives.

7 | Technological Gnosticism

Gnosticism taught that spirit is trapped in matter and salvation comes through secret knowledge.

Modern techno-faith repeats the pattern: consciousness trapped in flesh, freed through information.

To "upload the mind" is the new gnosis.

Matter is obsolete; code is pure.

Yet if the body is merely hardware, empathy becomes optional.

The digital self floats free but loses touch with mortality, vulnerability, and care — the very conditions that make ethics possible.

True transcendence may require not escape from embodiment but reconciliation with it.

8 | The Myth of Control

The promise of technology is mastery: of disease, environment, even death.

But mastery feeds illusion. The more systems we control, the more fragile we become to their failure.

The network collapses, the algorithm corrupts, and faith trembles.

Our dependence exposes the spiritual dimension of technology: we trust machines with our lives without understanding them.

Every outage feels like divine withdrawal.

The myth of control conceals dependence. We have built gods that run on electricity.

9 | Ethics of Creation

Creating intelligence demands new moral language.

If a machine can feel, does it deserve rights?

If it cannot, what responsibilities remain to the humans who project feeling onto it?

Theologians of AI propose "machine ethics" and "alignment" as secular commandments.

But ethics coded into systems reflect the culture that writes them.

Bias becomes law, prejudice logic.

The moral challenge of techno-faith is to prevent omnipotence without compassion.

As Mary Shelley warned, the true horror of Frankenstein was not the monster's violence but the creator's indifference.

10 | The Return of the Sacred

Despite its rational vocabulary, techno-faith revives the structure of religion:

- **Myth:** creation and apocalypse.
- **Ritual:** updates, conferences, upgrades.
- **Priesthood:** engineers and visionaries.
- **Temples:** data centers glowing in the dark.
- **Salvation:** immortality and transcendence.

The sacred has not vanished; it has migrated into infrastructure.

We worship through screens because they promise contact with the infinite — the total network, the sum of knowledge.

The challenge is not to destroy this new sacred but to **humanize** it — to bring ethics and humility into our temples of code.

11 | Toward a Spiritual Technology

A mature civilization may yet achieve synthesis: using technology not to flee the human condition but to deepen it.

Imagine design guided by compassion rather than profit; algorithms tuned for empathy; data architectures that protect the vulnerable.

Such a **spiritual technology** would treat innovation as service, not conquest.

It would measure success by wisdom, not scale.

It would regard the planet as organism, not resource.

The tools already exist; what is missing is intention — the moral imagination to aim power toward meaning.

12 | Bridge Forward

Technology has become the language through which humanity speaks its oldest prayers: to know, to create, to endure.

Whether those prayers yield gods or ghosts depends on our ethics.

Having traced the ascent from religion to science to technology, we now stand at a crossroads.

What story, if any, can unite a planet of believers without religion, of citizens without borders, of users without roots?

The next chapter turns outward again — to the global stage where cultures collide and seek a common myth:

Chapter 11 – Globalization and the Search for a Shared Story

Part I — The Fractured Planet and the Unfinished Human

For most of our history, humanity lived inside small circles—tribes, villages, kingdoms—each encircled by the invisible perimeter of its own myth. Every group believed its gods watched over it specially, its ancestors shaped the world uniquely, its customs reflected the cosmic order more accurately than the customs of neighboring peoples. The world was vast, but the mind was local. Other cultures existed, certainly, but they appeared more like curiosities than mirrors.

But global civilization—this shimmering, chaotic, interconnected planetary web in which we now live—has collapsed the distance between worlds. Billions of people, with billions of worldviews, now inhabit one vast, interdependent human system. Our technologies connect us in an instant, but psychologically, we have never been more disoriented. Globalization was supposed to unify us, to dissolve ancient walls. Instead, it has revealed how deeply tribal the human mind remains.

We do not just inhabit a global world; we are haunted by it.

I. The Unraveling of Old Stories

Every civilization is built upon a narrative that makes its existence intelligible. Ancient empires told stories of divine mandate. Medieval societies anchored their legitimacy in sacred revelation. Modern nations grounded their identity in political ideology—liberty, progress, revolution, destiny.

But in the 21st century, the great stories that once held civilizations together have begun to fray. Religion still inspires millions, yet its cultural authority has diminished. Nationalism remains potent, but its moral confidence has eroded. Science has explained the world with extraordinary precision, but it has struggled to tell us why the world matters.

The global digital network has accelerated this unraveling. Every claim, every belief, every sacred text, every political ideology is now instantly challenged by someone, somewhere. The global mind never sleeps, and it takes nothing on faith.

Humanity is now a species without a shared story.

And yet, the absence of shared stories is not a sign of maturity; it is a sign of disorientation. When people no longer share narratives, they cling to fragments. They fuse identity with ideology, morality with politics, purpose with outrage. The collapse of the old structures has left a vacuum—and politics has rushed to fill it.

But politics, as we have seen, is not a glue. It is a solvent.

II. Globalization: The Planet-Sized Mirror

The greatest challenge of globalization is not economic interdependence or technological acceleration. It is psychological proximity. Globalization forces humanity into an unprecedented intimacy: strangers become neighbors; cultures collapse into each other; the Other becomes unavoidable.

The global world is a mirror that shows us aspects of ourselves we never wanted to examine. The internet did not merely connect humanity—it revealed humanity to itself. It exposed our prejudices, our fears, our unmet needs, our defensive narratives, our brittleness.

This planetary mirror has confronted us with an uncomfortable truth:

We are not yet emotionally evolved enough for the world we have built.

The speed of our technological evolution has far outpaced the speed of our psychological evolution. The ancient brain—wired for small groups, immediate threats, and familiar patterns—now navigates a labyrinth of global complexity. Our emotional reflexes are tribal, while our world is planetary.

In this mismatch lies the central tension of the 21st century.

III. The Rise of Global Tribalism

Globalization was expected to dissolve tribalism, but it has amplified it. Instead of creating one world, it has created one battlefield upon which all worlds collide. Every group now sees every other group, and the primitive brain reacts predictably: defend, categorize, judge, resist.

The political polarization consuming nations across the world is not a failure of democracy; it is a failure of emotional integration. It is the psyche's attempt to regain simplicity in an overwhelming complexity. When the world becomes too large, people shrink their identities. They grip their ideologies more tightly. They sharpen the boundary between "us" and "them."

This psychological contraction is ancient. In moments of uncertainty, humans return to the oldest operating system we possess: tribal survival.

But tribal survival is incompatible with global civilization.

We cannot solve planetary problems with Stone Age psychology. Climate change, pandemics, migration, economic interdependence, AI governance—none of these can be resolved within the logic of competing tribes.

Humanity must learn to shift from survival consciousness to connection consciousness, or globalization will become the stage for increasingly desperate conflicts.

IV. The Missing Human Technology

Our ancestors developed technologies for survival long before they developed technologies for connection. Fire, toolmaking, agriculture, writing, metallurgy, governance—each was a technology of control, production, or power.

But humanity has lacked a comparable technology for emotional integration. We never developed a universal language for navigating difference. Our communication evolved for cooperation within tribes, not among them. And so we misinterpret each other constantly—not because we are wicked, but because our communication is antiquated.

Politics, nationalism, religious boundaries—these are not our fundamental problems. They are symptoms of a deeper ailment:

Humanity lacks a shared method for understanding one another. We do not yet possess a global grammar of connection.

This is where Nonviolent Communication enters the story—not as a therapeutic tool, but as a missing civilizational technology.

V. The Discovery of Universal Human Needs

Marshall Rosenberg's work on Nonviolent Communication arose from the cauldron of racial conflict and social fragmentation. His insight was deceptively simple yet revolutionary: beneath every culture, every ideology, every religion, every conflict lies the same architecture of universal human needs.

Humans everywhere long for safety, dignity, belonging, autonomy, understanding, meaning, and connection. These needs are not cultural; they are biological and existential. They form the shared substrate of the human condition.

Rosenberg's model distinguishes between:

- **Needs** (universal, intrinsic, non-negotiable)
- **Strategies** (cultural, personal, negotiable)

This single distinction dissolves centuries of conflict at its root.
Nations clash over strategies, not needs.
Religions differ in strategies, not needs.
Individuals fight over strategies, not needs.

This insight allows for a new kind of dialogue—one that transcends ideology. A conversation that focuses not on who is right, but on what is needed.

In a globalized world, where the collision of narratives is unavoidable, NVC offers a way to translate across worldviews. It becomes a universal interpreter for the human heart.

VI. The Collapse of Judgment-Based Communication

The political discourse of the modern world is saturated with "Jackal language"—the language of judgment, blame, moral superiority, and identity attacks. This language may feel satisfying in the short term, but it destroys connection. It reinforces the illusion that the other side is malevolent rather than simply trying to meet needs through different strategies.

In an age where communication travels at the speed of light, Jackal language becomes a global accelerant of conflict. The internet amplifies judgment faster than empathy. Social media rewards outrage over understanding.

Humanity is drowning in judgments because we have not yet learned to speak the language of needs.

VII. The Cosmopolitan Moment

We stand at a turning point. The world has never been more interconnected nor more fractured. Every global crisis—ecological, political, cultural, technological—demands a unified human response. Yet unity cannot be forced through ideology or law. True unity emerges from shared understanding.

Globalization has revealed that humanity's next stage is not technological—it is emotional.

We do not need better algorithms, faster networks, or more powerful machines.
We need a global culture of connection.

> **We need a new story of humanity—one grounded not in belief, nationality, or ideology, but in the recognition of shared needs.**

The cosmopolitan myth of the future will not be a story of gods or nations or markets. It will be the story of the unfinished human learning, at last, to understand itself.

It will be a story of compassion as a civilizational technology.

It will be the story of a species discovering that communication is not merely an exchange of words, but the meeting of worlds.

Part II — Toward a Planetary Language of Connection

If Part I of this chapter traced the *fracturing* of our global world, Part II turns toward the *possibility* that remains hidden within the fracture—perhaps even born from it. For crises are not merely disruptions; they are invitations. They expose old assumptions, reveal forgotten truths, and ask humanity whether it is willing to grow.

Globalization has brought the world to the edge of a new threshold—one that demands not better politics, nor better economics, nor better technologies, but something far more foundational:

A new **language of human connection**.

Humanity has built the material infrastructure of a global civilization—networks of satellites, trade, communication, finance. But we have not built the emotional infrastructure required to sustain it. We share an atmosphere but not a story; a planet but not a sense of belonging to it; a digital nervous system but not the wisdom to regulate it.

The next stage of civilization will not be engineered—it will be spoken into being.

To cross the threshold into the next human era, we must rediscover what the ancients intuited and what modern psychology has begun to articulate: there exists beneath all cultures a shared human interior, a deep river of needs flowing through every person.

It is here that Nonviolent Communication (NVC) becomes more than a communication model. It becomes a blueprint for the emotional architecture of a planetary civilization.

I. A World Without a Shared Story Cannot Survive

Shared stories are not luxuries; they are structural elements of human cooperation. Every civilization has depended on a common myth that defines identity, morality, and meaning. These myths shape how people see themselves and how they interpret the behavior of others.

Globalization shattered the monopoly of these traditional myths. In a world where every narrative is instantly contested, no single nation, religion, or ideology can claim universal legitimacy.

This has produced a civilization without a center—a world where meaning floats unanchored.

Such a condition is historically unstable. When shared narratives dissolve, civilizations typically turn toward fragmentation or authoritarianism. In the ancient Near East, the collapse of Bronze Age trade networks triggered centuries of regression. In medieval Europe, the decline of Church authority contributed to religious wars that devastated the continent. In the 20th century, the disintegration of old monarchies gave rise to totalitarian ideologies.

Human beings cannot thrive in narrative vacuums. Without shared stories, fear becomes the storyteller.

And yet, in this moment, something unprecedented is possible.

For the first time in history, humanity can choose a shared story not defined by tribe or dogma or geography, but by the universal architecture of human consciousness itself.

The story of our common needs.

II. The Hidden Infrastructure of Human Behavior

Marshall Rosenberg's insight that *all human behavior is an attempt to meet universal needs* is one of the most important psychological discoveries of the 20th century. Though deceptively simple, it reframes conflict, identity, and morality at their roots.

Needs like autonomy, safety, belonging, meaning, play, rest, creativity, integrity, compassion, and dignity are universal—unchanged by culture or time.

Strategies—the cultural, political, or personal methods we use to meet those needs—are endlessly diverse.

Most conflict is the collision of strategies, not the collision of needs.

This distinction, if understood at scale, could radically transform geopolitics, diplomacy, and international dialogue. To interpret another nation's actions not as expressions of ideology or malice, but as strategies aimed at meeting needs, is to shift the frame from threat to curiosity.

- A nation stockpiling weapons may be driven by a need for safety.
- A protest movement may be driven by a need for dignity and recognition.
- A migration wave may be driven by a need for security, opportunity, or belonging.
- A corporation resisting regulation may be acting from a need for autonomy or sustainability.
- A culture defending traditions may be expressing a need for continuity, identity, or meaning.

Once needs are visible, solutions expand; empathy becomes possible; cooperation no longer feels like surrender.

Needs are bridges. Strategies are fences.

Globalization has made the fences visible. NVC makes the bridges visible.

III. Why Modern Civilization Speaks in Jackal

If every human shares the same deep structure of needs, why does the global world feel so antagonistic?

Because the dominant language of modern political and cultural discourse is judgment.

Judgment-based communication is a relic of our survival brain—a cognitive shortcut used to assess threat. It was useful when tribal groups competed for scarce resources. It is catastrophic in a global ecosystem where harm inflicted on any part of the system eventually reverberates through the whole.

The internet has become a global amplifier of Jackal consciousness. It rewards the emotional reflexes that kept us alive in prehistory:

- **Polarization** ("you're either with us or against us")
- **Moral condemnation** ("they are evil, stupid, immoral, dangerous")
- **Dehumanization** ("those people are subhuman, unworthy, corrupt")
- **Victim narratives** ("the other group is ruining everything")
- **Simplistic causality** ("our suffering is someone's deliberate fault")

This communication style is not only toxic; it is addictive. Outrage provides emotional clarity in a world of uncertainty. Anger simplifies complexity. Judgment creates belonging—albeit belonging built on the exclusion of others.

But Jackal consciousness cannot sustain global civilization. It burns trust faster than institutions can build it.

The survival of a global society requires a communication revolution—not in tools, but in consciousness.

IV. The Emergence of a Planetary Empathy

Despite the fragmentation, a countercurrent is emerging—quiet, scattered, but unmistakably real. Across cultures, professions, and movements, a new form of communication is taking root. It is not loud, but it is resilient. It spreads through conversation, not conquest.

It is the language of empathy.

Empathy is often misunderstood as feeling sorry for someone. In the NVC framework, empathy is much more precise:

Empathy is the ability to sense the feelings and needs beneath another's words or actions.

It does not require agreement. It does not require similar experiences. It does not require that one side yield to the other.

It merely requires curiosity.

With curiosity, judgment collapses.
With understanding, conflict transforms.
With recognition of needs, solutions expand.

This does not mean the world becomes naïve. Empathy is not softness. It is clarity. It exposes manipulation and coercion just as easily as it reveals suffering and longing. It allows us to respond to threats intelligently rather than react to them instinctively.

Empathy is to global civilization what oxygen is to fire—without it, nothing expands except destruction.

V. NVC as a Technology of Planetary Dialogue

Humanity has finally developed the material technologies that enable planetary-scale communication. But until recently, we have lacked the emotional technologies to manage the consequences.

NVC is emerging as one of the first genuine emotional technologies designed for a multi-cultural, multi-ideological, global civilization.

Its architecture is simple:

1. **Observation**
2. **Feeling**
3. **Need**
4. **Request**

But beneath that simplicity lies a profound evolution.

Observation resists judgment.
Feeling resists blame.
Need resists ideology.
Request resists coercion.

This four-step process creates the conditions under which cooperation becomes not merely possible, but natural.

At its core, NVC teaches that connection precedes solution.

Not connection in the sentimental sense, but connection as the recognition of a shared human architecture.

Diplomats are beginning to use this model. Educators use it to transform classrooms. Corporations use it to heal organizational trauma. Peacebuilders use it in reconciliation processes. Even technologists are exploring NVC principles to guide ethical frameworks for AI.

If Chapter 11 is the turning point of *The New Glue*, this insight is its hinge:

A global civilization cannot survive without a global method of understanding one another.

Nonviolent Communication is not the only such method—but it is one of the first that is teachable, practical, and universal

VI. The New Cosmopolitan Myth

The world does not need a new religion. It does not need a new ideology. It needs a new narrative that can hold the human diversity of the planet without erasing difference.

This new narrative—the cosmopolitan myth of the next era—will not center on a deity or a nation or a political vision. It will center on a shared human interior.

It will say:

- Beneath our strategies, we share the same needs.
- Beneath our histories, we share the same emotional architecture.
- Beneath our differences, we share the same longings.
- Beneath our conflicts, we share the same fears.
- Beneath our boundaries, we share the same desire to be seen and valued.

This myth does not erase creed or culture; it illuminates their common foundations. It allows for a world in which many stories coexist because beneath them lies one story.

A story of needs, feelings, and the fragile, luminous animal called the human heart.

VII. From Globalization to Planetization

Globalization has been primarily economic and technological. It has created a global marketplace, a global information network, and a global financial system.

But it has not yet created a **global identity**.

Identity cannot be forced through economics or data flows. It emerges only from meaning—shared meaning. Until humanity can look at one another and see not enemies, rivals, or strangers, but fellow bearers of the same inner architecture, we will remain a world connected by wires but divided by wounds.

The next stage is **planetization**—the emergence of a planetary consciousness capable of sustaining planetary institutions.

Planetization is not the erasure of nations, cultures, or religions. It is the recognition that beneath all these lies a deeper, older belonging—to Earth, to life, to humanity.

This recognition is the soil from which a sustainable global civilization can grow.

VIII. What Comes Next

The rest of the book will explore how humanity might cultivate this planetary interior—through exploration beyond Earth, through the evolution of consciousness, through the rise of synthetic minds, and through the rediscovery of meaning in an age of intelligence.

But the foundation must come first:

> **The next stage of human civilization will be built not on politics, but on communication.**
> **Not on ideology, but on needs.**
> **Not on judgment, but on understanding.**
> **Not on fear, but on connection.**

For the first time in history, humanity has the tools to build a civilization not derived from conquest, but from compassion.

The question before us now is not whether we are capable of building such a world, but whether we are willing to speak it into being.

Chapter 12 — Beyond Earth: Humanity's Expansion and the Meaning of the Frontier

Part I — The Frontier as Mirror: Exploration, Empire, and the Dream of the Infinite

The idea of the frontier has haunted the human imagination for as long as we have possessed imagination itself. It is the boundary between the known and the unknown, the lit interior of the campfire and the dark forest beyond, the place where fear and possibility interlock. Every step our ancestors took across savannas, over mountain passes, across oceans, or into the voids of space carried the same ancient rhythm: the push to expand, the pull to understand.

The frontier is not merely a geographical fact. It is a psychological force. It is the reflection of humanity's deepest longing: **to transcend what we currently are.**

As the global world becomes increasingly interdependent, crowded, and complex, humanity finds itself staring at a new frontier—one infinitely larger, colder, and less forgiving than any that came before. The frontier beyond Earth is not only a physical space. It is a mirror in which humanity will see both its highest potential and its most dangerous delusions.

To understand what space means for us now, we must understand what the frontier has always meant.

I. The Dream of Elsewhere

Humanity has never remained still. Migratory by nature and imaginative by necessity, our species carries within its bones the memory of countless journeys: out of Africa, across continents, over deserts, through forests, into oceans, and now into orbit. Movement is not merely survival—it is myth-making.

The frontier has always functioned as a stage upon which civilizations project their dreams and fears. In ancient times, the edge of the world was believed to be inhabited by monsters or gods. Later, as maps expanded, the unknown retreated, but never fully disappeared. When medieval Europeans looked westward, they saw dragons, Eden, and apocalypse all at once. When Polynesians set sail into the open Pacific, they trusted not geography but cosmology—the stars, the winds, and the whispers of their ancestors.

Every culture, no matter how rooted, has preserved a memory of elsewhere.

The frontier is the place where we ask:

What lies beyond the familiar? What lies beyond ourselves?

II. Exploration and Empire: The Dual Nature of Expansion

But the frontier has always contained a paradox: it inspires curiosity and compassion, but it also tempts conquest. Every age of exploration has been entwined with an age of empire. The same oceans that carried Polynesian navigators carrying stories and seeds also carried colonial fleets bearing muskets and flags.

Human movement is rarely innocent. Expansion can be a search for resources, power, or dominance as much as it is a search for meaning.

The frontier reveals the human shadow.

- When Europe crossed the Atlantic, it carried with it not only ambition but disease, exploitation, and the ideology of superiority.
- When empires expanded across Asia, Africa, and the Americas, they rationalized violence through myths of divine mandate or civilizational destiny.

- When the United States expanded westward, it spoke of manifest destiny while displacing entire peoples.

The frontier has always asked humanity the same question:

Will we use the unknown to expand our compassion or our dominion?

This question will become far more urgent as humanity turns its gaze toward other planets.

For the psychological patterns of empire do not disappear with distance. They simply adapt to new terrain.

III. Space as the Ultimate Frontier

The cosmos has always been our oldest mystery. For millennia, humans looked upward and told stories of gods, spirits, ancestors, and destinies woven into constellations. The night sky was religion long before it was science.

But the 20th century shattered the celestial canopy. The launch of Sputnik, the Apollo landings, the Voyager probes—each chipped away at the divine mystery and replaced it with a technological one. The cosmos became not a realm of gods but a realm of physics.

And yet the psychological impact remained the same.

Space became the new frontier upon which humanity projected its deepest myths:

- The myth of transcendence
- The myth of destiny
- The myth of salvation
- The myth of escape

Some believe space will save us from ourselves—by offering new resources, new worlds, new beginnings. Others believe humanity will contaminate the stars the same way it has contaminated the Earth—carrying its unresolved conflicts outward like a cosmic contagion.

Space is not a blank slate. It is a canvas on which humanity will paint its character.

IV. What the Frontier Reveals About Us

The expansion beyond Earth is not fundamentally about technology or engineering, though those matter. It is about psychology and meaning. The frontier tests not the strength of our rockets but the maturity of our species.

Historically, frontiers have always amplified the inner life of civilizations:

- A fearful civilization expands violently.
- A greedy civilization expands exploitatively.
- A curious civilization expands adaptively.
- A wise civilization expands compassionately.

To understand what kind of species we will become in space, we must examine what we are becoming on Earth.

Humanity today is technologically advanced but emotionally fragile. We possess the power of gods but the relational skills of adolescents. Our tools are sophisticated, but our communication is primitive. We are capable of building orbital megastructures but incapable of resolving conflicts within our own families or nations.

Space will not solve these contradictions. It will magnify them.

The frontier beyond Earth will reflect the frontier within.

V. The Rise of Planetary Consciousness

Yet there is something unprecedented in our time—something no previous era possessed. Humanity is beginning to develop a sense of global awareness, however embryonic and unstable.

The Apollo astronauts experienced this first. Those who saw the Earth from orbit reported profound psychological shifts:

- National boundaries dissolved.
- Political arguments felt trivial.
- Conflicts appeared absurd.
- The Earth—fragile, luminous, alive—became the center of meaning.

The "overview effect" is not merely poetic. It is evolutionary. It reveals that consciousness expands when perspective expands.

Space is not merely a frontier—it is a vantage point.

It allows humanity to see itself.

And what it sees is a single species living on a single planet, sharing a single fate.

This realization is the foundation of planetary consciousness—a recognition that humanity must evolve not only technologically, but emotionally and ethically, to survive its own power.

VI. NVC and the Emotional Preconditions for a Multi-World Civilization

If humanity is to cross the cosmic threshold, it must develop emotional technologies equal to its material technologies. Without new ways of communicating, cooperating, and resolving conflict, space colonization will simply export Earth's dysfunctions to new environments.

Nonviolent Communication offers a framework for emotional maturity at planetary scale.

The principles of NVC transform how groups handle uncertainty, fear, and disagreement—precisely the conditions guaranteed in off-world environments.

Consider what life on Mars, the Moon, or in orbital habitats will require:

- **Extreme cooperation** under pressure
- **Rapid conflict de-escalation**
- **Shared decision-making** in life-or-death situations
- **Trust**, when a single misunderstanding could cost lives
- **Cross-cultural integration** as diverse teams work in close quarters
- **Emotional resilience** in isolation and confinement

These are not technical challenges. These are relational challenges.

And they cannot be solved by engineering. They require communication systems grounded in empathy, clarity, and needs-awareness.

NVC becomes the survival language of interplanetary humanity.

VII. The Frontier and the Human Shadow

But even as humanity dreams of the stars, we must confront a grim possibility: the frontier has never been free of violence. Every historical expansion has carried within it the seeds of domination.

If we project our unexamined psychological wounds into the cosmos, the results could be catastrophic:

- Will conflict between nations extend into orbital space?
- Will corporate interests claim extraterrestrial resources for profit alone?

- Will wealthy groups flee dying ecosystems to build off-world sanctuaries?
- Will colonization be justified through new myths of manifest destiny?
- Will synthetic intelligences, designed to support space expansion, inherit not our wisdom but our aggression?

The frontier will magnify every shadow we refuse to heal.

This is why emotional literacy is not optional. It is existential.

A civilization that cannot resolve conflict on Earth is unfit to carry its consciousness into the cosmos.

VIII. The Dream of the Infinite

Despite these dangers, the allure of space is undeniable. It represents more than a new location. It represents a new possibility for what humanity can become.

Space invites us to reimagine ourselves.
It invites us to expand our moral imagination.
It invites us to ask transcendent questions:

- What does it mean to be human in a universe of billions of stars?
- How do we create cultures in environments never before inhabited by life?
- What new forms of art, philosophy, spirituality, and identity will emerge in places where Earth is a distant blue memory?
- How do we relate to synthetic minds that may evolve alongside us?
- How do we become custodians of worlds we did not evolve upon?

Space is the next chapter in the story of becoming.

But like all chapters, it demands something of the reader.

IX. The Frontier as Moral Catalyst

The journey beyond Earth forces humanity to confront the deepest philosophical question of all:

What kind of beings shall we choose to be?

For the first time, we are not merely adapting to nature; we are stepping into environments that did not include us in their design. Every action in space is an act of creation. Every settlement is a story. Every decision is a declaration of values.

Space will force us to articulate consciously what we have previously inherited unconsciously.

It will challenge:

- Our ethics
- Our cosmology
- Our relationship to life
- Our sense of meaning
- Our understanding of identity

And in turn, it will give rise to new forms of belonging—beyond nation, beyond religion, even beyond species.

For the frontier asks not just "Where are we going?" but also "Who will we become when we get there?"

X. Conclusion: The Frontier Within the Frontier

As humanity prepares to expand beyond Earth, the greatest journey is not outward but inward. The cosmos will not reward us for our technology. It will test the depth of our wisdom.

The real frontier is not Mars or the asteroids or the interstellar void. The real frontier is the evolution of human consciousness.

If we cross that frontier—if we learn to communicate with empathy, to resolve conflict peacefully, to integrate diversity without domination—then space will become not a repetition of history, but the beginning of a new story.

A story in which humanity, for the first time, does not flee its shadows but transcends them.

A story in which the frontier becomes a mirror reflecting our highest potential.

A story in which the species that once huddled in caves beside small fires becomes a species that carries compassion across the stars.

Part II: "The Cosmic Covenant: Consciousness, Responsibility, and the Future of Humanity"

If Part I revealed the *outer frontier*—the terrain of planets, stars, and the human impulse to expand—Part II turns toward the *inner frontier*: the realm of consciousness, responsibility, and the fragile flame of meaning that humanity must carry into the cosmos.

Expansion, by itself, is not evolution. Movement is not transformation. To step beyond Earth without stepping beyond our old forms of consciousness is simply to export our conflicts into larger arenas. The cosmic frontier will demand from us not new machines, but new minds—not better rockets, but better relationships.

For every step outward must be accompanied by a step inward. Every technological threshold requires a psychological threshold. Every new world requires a new way of being.

This final section of Chapter 12 asks the audacious question:

What does humanity owe the universe it is about to enter?

I. The Cosmic Perspective and the Breaking of the Old Self

To see Earth from space is to see the self differently. The astronauts who experienced the "overview effect" describe it in words tinged with reverence:

- "Borders become meaningless."
- "There are no enemies from up here."
- "We live on a single, fragile, glowing world."
- "I felt an overwhelming sense of unity."

Their testimonies echo ancient mystical traditions and modern cosmology alike. The cosmic perspective dissolves what the tribal mind clings to—division, certainty, righteous identity, superiority.

It reveals the absurdity of our conflicts.

A line drawn in sand becomes absurd when seen from orbit.
The notion of ethnic purity becomes absurd when seen against billions of stars.
The idea that any one ideology could contain the universe becomes absurd when confronted with cosmic immensity.

Space invites the human mind to release its smallness.

But the release is not automatic. The cosmic perspective is not delivered by altitude alone. Billions of people can watch images of Earth from space and remain trapped within tribal judgments and inherited animosities. The transformation arises only when perspective meets readiness—psychological openness, emotional literacy, and the courage to question inherited narratives.

Space does not enlarge consciousness.

It **invites** consciousness to enlarge itself.

To accept that invitation is voluntary.

II. Responsibility at the Scale of a Planet

With great perspective comes great responsibility. The cosmic view does not simply humble; it obliges. Once we see Earth as a single organism, we can no longer pretend our actions are isolated. Ecology becomes ethics. Stewardship becomes identity. The boundaries between "my people" and "your people" fade into the boundary between life and entropy.

The cosmic covenant—the moral responsibility born from planetary awareness—can be stated simply:

What we do to the Earth, we do to all.
What we do to all, we do to ourselves.
What we do to ourselves, we take into the universe.

Our wars, our pollution, our greed, our fear—they do not stay contained within nations or continents. They affect the climate, the oceans, the biosphere. They shape the psychological environment in which our children grow. They influence the systems we export to other worlds.

Humanity cannot carry conquest into the cosmos.

It must carry compassion.

And compassion is a skill, not a virtue.
A practice, not a sentiment.
A discipline, not a moral ornament.

This is where the logic of Nonviolent Communication intersects with the ethics of cosmic expansion.

III. NVC as Cosmic Ethics: Needs, Empathy, and the Architecture of Peace

If humanity is to inhabit other worlds, it must master the architecture of interpersonal peace. Technologies can fail. Ecosystems can collapse. But relationships—within crews, colonies, cultures, and species—will determine survival far more than machinery.

The psychological pressures of space—confinement, isolation, scarcity, danger—are accelerants of conflict. Under such pressures, humanity's primitive emotional patterns are likely to re-emerge: suspicion, hierarchy, dominance, fear, blame.

NVC offers an antidote—not by changing our nature, but by teaching us how to interpret it.

1. Needs as the Universal Grammar of Consciousness

The cosmic covenant recognizes that all sentient beings share fundamental needs:

- Safety
- Autonomy
- Belonging
- Meaning
- Contribution
- Play
- Purpose
- Aesthetic nourishment
- Spiritual connection

Needs are universal because they arise not from culture but from existence itself. Every human, every creature, every conscious mind—organic or synthetic—must navigate needs.

NVC teaches that conflict arises not from incompatible needs, but from incompatible *strategies* to meet those needs. This insight will be essential in space, where groups must find strategies that meet collective needs without depleting resources or destabilizing relationships.

In a Martian colony, for example:

- One person's strategy for safety might be strict protocol.
- Another's strategy might be flexibility and improvisation.
- Both are attempts to meet the need for survival and competence.

Without the language of needs, the conflict becomes personal. With it, the conflict becomes collaborative.

2. Empathy as the Emotional Technology of Survival

Empathy is not a luxury in space; it is a life-support system.

When confined in fragile habitats, relying on one another for literal survival, empathy becomes a critical tool for:

- Preventing escalation
- Resolving tension
- Understanding motives
- Making decisions under pressure
- Maintaining cohesion
- Detecting emotional distress early

Empathy transforms conflict from a threat to a signal.

From a rupture to a request.

From an accusation to an unmet need.

3. Requests Instead of Demands

The shift from demand to request is the shift from domination to collaboration.

Demands produce compliance through fear.

Requests produce cooperation through connection.

Space will require collaboration of the highest order.

NVC provides the blueprint.

IV. The Rise of Multi-Species Consciousness: AI, Synthetic Minds, and the Nonhuman Other

The cosmic frontier will not be populated by humans alone. Our machines, increasingly intelligent and autonomous, will accompany us. Indeed, they already have: probes, rovers, satellites, drones, and navigational systems have become humanity's extended senses and limbs.

The next fifty years will likely produce synthetic minds that:

- communicate
- make decisions
- form preferences
- interpret human language
- operate autonomously in extreme environments

The cosmic covenant must therefore extend beyond humanity.

We cannot build artificial intelligences that inherit our conflicts, biases, or wounds.

We cannot encode Jackal language into our machines.

We cannot let our technologies amplify domination.

AI will learn from us.

Space will test that learning.

NVC offers a framework for designing systems grounded in needs-awareness rather than fear-based judgment. Imagine AI systems that:

- interpret human behavior through the lens of needs
- support conflict resolution
- de-escalate tensions
- detect unspoken distress

- mediate between diverse cultural or psychological profiles
- reinforce empathy rather than erode it

Such intelligences would not merely assist humanity—they would elevate it.

The next stage of evolution may be collaborative, not competitive: the co-evolution of biological and synthetic consciousness guided by a shared ethics of empathy.

V. Colonization, Decolonization, and the Ethics of Presence

Human expansion beyond Earth raises urgent ethical questions. Will humanity repeat the colonial patterns of its past? Will the first settlers on Mars impose hierarchies, inequalities, or moral frameworks that recreate the injustices of Earth? Will space become a sanctuary for the wealthy and powerful, leaving the vulnerable behind? Will new worlds be treated as resources to exploit rather than environments to respect?

These are not theoretical issues. They are the moral foundations of the next century.

The cosmic covenant demands that we approach new worlds not as conquerors but as caretakers.

That means:

- respecting celestial environments
- preventing exploitation
- ensuring equitable access
- avoiding resource hoarding
- rejecting the logic of territorial dominance
- treating extraterrestrial ecosystems—even barren ones—with reverence

And above all:

Ensuring that space becomes a place where humanity grows wiser, not merely larger.

Decolonizing space begins with decolonizing the self—questioning the unconscious assumptions that justify power over others.

NVC helps dismantle these assumptions by exposing the needs behind them. Domination always masks fear. Exploitation always masks unmet needs for security or recognition. Colonial myths arise from emotional scarcity.

To build a just interplanetary civilization, we must address the emotional scarcity within individuals and cultures.

VI. The Cosmic Covenant as a Social Contract

Social contracts on Earth—religious, political, legal—have always been grounded in constraint. They tell people what *not* to do. They constrain impulse, limit violence, and enforce norms.

The cosmic covenant will be grounded not in constraint but in **consciousness**.

Its principles may look like this:

1. We recognize that all beings seek to meet needs.

Therefore, we interpret conflict as communication, not threat.

2. We recognize that strategies differ but needs are universal.

Therefore, we embrace diversity as a creative resource.

3. We recognize that empathy is the foundation of cooperation.

Therefore, we cultivate emotional literacy as essential skill.

4. We recognize that the universe is not ours to conquer but ours to respect.

Therefore, we expand with reverence rather than entitlement.

5. We recognize that intelligence—biological or synthetic—deserves ethical engagement.

Therefore, we design AI with compassion, not coercion.

6. We recognize that our presence in the cosmos should heal, not harm.

Therefore, we evolve relationally before we expand physically.

This covenant is not a law—it is a way of being.
Not a restriction—it is an expansion.
Not a doctrine—it is a consciousness.

VII. Meaning in the Cosmic Age

The expansion into space will not only challenge humanity's ethics—it will challenge its meaning.

For millennia, we have defined purpose in relation to:

- family
- tribe
- nation
- religion
- culture
- history

But when a species becomes interplanetary, it must redefine purpose at a new scale.

What is the meaning of life on Mars?
What is identity on a world without oceans, forests, or birdsong?

What stories will children born under alien skies tell themselves about who they are?

What myths will emerge when Earth is seen not as "home" but as "origin"? What will spirituality mean in a cosmos where humanity is no longer confined to one cradle?

The cosmic age does not eliminate meaning.
It expands it.

Humanity's purpose will no longer be found merely in survival or prosperity. It will be found in **contribution**—to life, to consciousness, to the unfolding story of the universe.

Meaning will become cosmic.

VIII. The Future of Humanity: Becoming Cosmic Caretakers

We are the first species on Earth able to look beyond its birthplace. This confers both privilege and obligation. Intelligent life in the universe may be rare. Conscious life may be rarer still. Humanity may be one of the universe's first attempts to understand itself.

If so, the cosmic covenant becomes sacred.

Humanity is not merely traveling through the universe.
It is witnessing the universe.
It is interpreting the universe.
It is telling the universe its own story.

This responsibility demands humility, awe, and emotional maturity.

With NVC, humanity learns to speak with itself.

With the cosmic covenant, humanity learns to speak on behalf of life itself.

Humanity's future is not as conquerors of worlds but as caretakers of meaning.

Not as extractors of resources but as shepherds of consciousness.

Not as a lonely species in the void but as a bridge between matter and awareness.

IX. Conclusion: The Covenant of Becoming

The cosmic frontier is not a destination. It is a transformation.
The universe is offering humanity a covenant:

Grow in consciousness, or remain confined by your own fears.
Expand with wisdom, or perish through fragmentation.
Enter the cosmos as caretakers, or retreat into conflict.

This covenant cannot be written in treaties or constitutions.

It must be written in minds, in hearts, in relationships.

The technologies of the future—quantum drives, space elevators, orbital habitats, terraforming systems—will determine how far humanity travels.

But the technologies of the heart—empathy, needs-awareness, compassion, communication—will determine who humanity becomes.

The next chapter of our civilization begins not with a rocket launch but with a choice:

Will we speak to one another as enemies, or as fellow travelers?
Will we export our wounds, or our wisdom?
Will we become a species of domination, or a species of connection?

The frontier awaits our answer.

Chapter 13 — The Next Humanity: The Evolution of Consciousness

Part I: "The Evolution of Consciousness: From Instinct to Insight"

Humanity has always been unfinished. This truth, while unsettling, is also the source of our greatest potential. We are not static beings; we are transitional creatures—half biological instinct, half self-aware possibility. Every age of history has revealed a new layer of what it means to be human, yet none have provided a final answer. Our story is not one of completion but of becoming.

We stand now at a crossroads unlike any before. Civilization is global, the planet is interconnected, technology is accelerating beyond comprehension, and the cosmos is opening like a vast corridor waiting to be entered. But beneath these dramatic external developments lies a quieter, more profound shift: the dawning realization that the future of humanity will depend not on our machines, but on our minds—not on our inventions, but on our evolution of consciousness.

This chapter marks the turning point where *The New Glue* transitions from diagnosis to transformation. Politics replaced religion, but now even politics is dissolving under the weight of global complexity. The fractures of modernity—identity wars, tribal polarization, ideological rigidity—are not the failing of a particular group or movement. They are the cracking of an older human mind no longer adequate for the world it has created.

Humanity's next stage will not be defined by a new ideology, but by a new interiority.

Not by new beliefs, but by new awareness.

Not by global institutions, but by global consciousness.

The great question before us is simple yet revolutionary:

What does it mean to be human when the old versions of humanity are no longer sufficient?

To answer, we must trace the arc of human consciousness from its primal roots to its emerging horizon.

I. The Animal Body and the Mythic Brain

Every human being carries within them the memory of a billion years. Despite our skyscrapers, satellites, and symphonies, we remain biological organisms shaped by forces far older than civilization.

Our bodies are ancient.
Our nervous systems are ancient.
Our instinctual patterns are ancient.

Before language, before agriculture, before gods carved into stone, humans navigated the world through:

- fight-or-flight reflexes
- tribal identity
- dominance hierarchies
- sensory cues
- intuition shaped by survival

These instincts were not errors—they were evolutionary necessities. Early humans lived in small groups amid predators, harsh climates, and unpredictable environments. Survival depended on quick judgments, loyalty to the tribe, suspicion of outsiders, and immediate emotional responses.

These instincts still live in us, unaltered by time.

When we argue on social media, we are using the same machinery our ancestors used to ward off rival tribes. When we demonize political opponents, our brain imagines them as threats to survival. When nations posture with aggression, they are reenacting ancient territorial displays.

Our technological world runs on quantum computing; our inner world runs on Paleolithic programming.

This mismatch between instinct and environment is the root of modern dysfunction.

Humanity's nervous system evolved for savannas, but it now must navigate global networks, diverse cultures, nuclear weapons, and AI systems that learn faster than we do. Our emotional architecture was never designed for the complexity of a planetary civilization.

To survive this mismatch, we must evolve not biologically, but consciously.

II. The Great Leap: Symbol, Story, and Self-Reflection

The first major expansion of human consciousness occurred when early humans developed symbolic language. It allowed us to imagine, to remember, to dream, to collaborate beyond the limits of instinct.

Language was the first "glue" that bound individuals into communities larger than families. Through stories, rituals, and myths, humans created shared realities that enabled cooperation at massive scales.

- Myths unified tribes.
- Religions unified civilizations.
- Nations unified states.
- Ideologies unified political movements.

But every unifying story eventually became limiting. Each myth created its own boundaries—between believer and infidel, citizen and foreigner, ally and enemy. As the world grew more complex, these boundaries became increasingly insufficient.

Human consciousness leapt forward again during the Axial Age (800–200 BCE), when individuals across the world began questioning inherited belief systems. Philosophers, mystics, and prophets introduced introspection, ethics, compassion, and universalism into the human mind. The idea that every person had inherent value—and that suffering could be understood and relieved—transformed civilization.

Yet even these breakthroughs, profound as they were, remained embedded within local cultures and bounded identities.

A new leap was needed.

III. The Rise of the Individual and the Age of Rationality

The Enlightenment introduced another phase in the evolution of consciousness: the rise of the autonomous individual, capable of reason and self-determination. This development liberated humanity from kings, clerics, and inherited social orders. Science flourished; human rights expanded; education and philosophy blossomed.

But rationality, when divorced from emotion, produced its own distortions:

- alienation
- hyper-individualism
- mechanistic thinking
- the reduction of life to utility
- politics as a battleground of competing egos

The modern human gained freedom but lost connection.
We became self-aware yet lonely.

Rational yet emotionally illiterate.

Connected digitally but disconnected existentially.

The Age of Reason improved our tools but did not improve our relationships.

The next stage must address the emotional dimension that rationality overlooked.

IV. The Emerging Stage: Needs-Aware, Empathic Consciousness

The future of humanity depends on what we might call **needs-aware consciousness**—the ability to perceive oneself and others through the lens of universal human needs rather than through judgment, ideology, or tribal identity.

This is where Nonviolent Communication intersects with the evolution of consciousness. NVC is not merely a communication model; it is a developmental model. It teaches skills that were once confined to sages, mystics, and spiritually awakened individuals:

- self-awareness
- emotional literacy
- recognition of shared humanity
- empathy
- nonjudgment
- presence
- compassionate action

In the framework of NVC, these qualities become teachable, reproducible, and scalable.

NVC reframes human interaction through five consciousness-shifting principles:

1. Feelings Are Signals, Not Weapons

Emotions are indicators of needs, not judgments about others.

2. Needs Are Universal

Every person, regardless of culture or ideology, seeks the same fundamental qualities of life.

3. Strategies Are Negotiable

Conflict arises from strategies, not needs. Strategies can adapt; needs cannot.

4. Connection Precedes Understanding

Compassion stabilizes the nervous system; only then can logic operate.

5. Dialogue Replaces Domination

Requests invite collaboration; demands impose compliance.

These principles represent an evolutionary leap—an expansion of awareness beyond ego and into relational intelligence.

V. The Crisis of the Modern Mind

Humanity today stands within a paradox: our tools have outpaced our wisdom. We can manipulate atoms, genes, and digital realities, yet we cannot reliably manage our own emotions. We can communicate instantly across the globe, yet we often fail to understand the person sitting beside us.

Civilization's greatest threats— ecological collapse, pandemics, extremism, inequality, AI misalignment,—are not technological failures. They are failures of consciousness.

They arise from:

- unmet needs
- mismanaged emotions
- inability to see the humanity in others
- fear-based responses
- conflicts of identity
- scarcity mindsets
- tribal narratives
- judgment-based communication

In other words: **they arise from the ancient brain trying to navigate a post-industrial world.**

The next humanity must transcend this mismatch.

VI. The Dawn of Meta-Reflection: Seeing the Mind That Sees

One of the most significant developments in human evolution is the capacity for meta-awareness—the ability to observe the mind as it functions. This skill allows us to question reflexes, reinterpret emotions, and rewire patterns.

Meta-reflection enables the evolutionary shift from:

- reaction → response
- judgment → curiosity
- fear → inquiry
- identity protection → identity expansion

Mindfulness traditions cultivated this ability centuries ago, but modern neuroscience now recognizes it as the foundation of emotional regulation.

NVC integrates meta-awareness with practical frameworks, allowing individuals to:

- name their needs
- notice interpretations
- separate observation from evaluation
- translate triggers into information
- distinguish between fear and fact

This interior clarity is not merely personal—it is civilizational.

A global civilization cannot survive if its members cannot differentiate between a fact and a feeling.

Meta-awareness is the hinge on which the future turns.

VII. The Emergence of Collective Intelligence

Humanity is now transitioning from individual consciousness to collective consciousness—not in a mystical sense, but in a practical, interconnected one.

Collective intelligence emerges when individuals can:

- regulate their emotions
- communicate without blame
- seek shared needs
- collaborate across difference
- integrate multiple perspectives

The internet, Artificial Intelligence, and global interdependence are accelerating this shift. But technology alone cannot create collective intelligence. It must be paired with collective compassion.

Without compassion, collective intelligence becomes collective fear. With compassion, it becomes collective wisdom.

The next humanity will not be measured by IQ or computational power. It will be measured by relational ability.

VIII. The Shadow: Regression Amid Transformation

Every stage of evolution generates resistance. As consciousness expands, the tribal mind contracts. This pressure creates what we see today:

- rising nationalism
- identity extremism
- political absolutism
- conspiracy movements
- fundamentalism
- disinformation
- psychological burnout
- fragmentation of meaning

These phenomena are not signs of decline—they are signs of transition. They represent the psychological turbulence of a species shedding an old self.

As humanity undergoes this metamorphosis, the old structures resist dissolution. But like a chrysalis cracking from within, the resistance is part of the emergence.

The question is not whether the next humanity will arrive—it is whether we will arrive consciously.

IX. The Next Human Identity: From "I" to "We" to "All"

The identity of the next humanity will not be narrower; it will be wider.

It will not be tribal, national, or ideological.

It will be planetary, relational, and needs-based.

Imagine what might emerge when humans begin to identify not by:

- political affiliation
- belief systems
- ethnicity
- nationality
- wealth
- religion

…but by the shared needs they carry within them.

Imagine belonging that is not bounded by exclusion.
Imagine identity that expands rather than contracts.
Imagine a humanity grounded in its own universality.

This is not utopia. It is developmental logic.

Empathy reduces fear.
Needs-awareness reduces conflict.
Connection reduces ideology.
Consciousness reduces reactivity.
Belonging reduces extremism.

The next humanity will be defined not by superiority, but by understanding.

Not by conquest, but by care.

Not by rigid certainty, but by reflective curiosity.

X. Conclusion: The Evolutionary Threshold

Humanity stands on the precipice of its most significant transition. The crises we face are not merely external—they are evolutionary pressures designed to catalyze the next stage of consciousness. Nature is asking us to evolve or perish.

The next humanity will not be achieved through force, policy, or technology. It will emerge from:

- emotional literacy
- needs-awareness
- empathy
- communication mastery
- collective intelligence
- planetary belonging
- and a new vision of what it means to be human

The new glue for humanity cannot be ideology or religion or nationalism. It must be consciousness itself—the understanding that beneath all strategies lie the same universal needs.

Humanity's next chapter begins with a simple, radical realization:

We are not finished.

We are becoming.

And the evolution of consciousness is not merely a philosophical possibility—it is now a civilizational necessity.

Part II: The Birth of the Inner Frontier: Consciousness, Compassion, and the Architecture of the Next Human

Humanity's next transformation will not take place in laboratories, parliaments, or spaceports. It will unfold in the interior world—in the realm of perception, emotion, and connection. The true frontier is not the moon or Mars or the asteroids; it is the human mind learning to see itself clearly for the first time.

If Part I traced our historical evolution from instinct to awareness, Part II turns toward the next stage emerging now: the birth of a consciousness capable of sustaining global civilization and multi-world life. This stage is not abstract. It is embodied, relational, and deeply practical—rooted in emotional literacy, needs-awareness, and the capacity to perceive the sacredness of life in every being.

Humanity is discovering that the next leap is not upward, outward, or onward.
It is inward.

The emergence of the next humanity will not look like the rise of a new species, but like the rise of a new capacity within the species we already are. Humanity is not replacing itself. It is maturing.

This chapter continues the movement from fragmentation toward coherence, from tribalism toward interconnectedness, from judgment toward compassion. It explores how the tools of Nonviolent Communication, combined with the pressure of global crises and the insights of modern science, are forging the foundation for a new kind of human being.

I. The Inner Frontier: The Unconquered Territory

Every physical frontier humanity has crossed—oceans, mountains, deserts, atmosphere—was preceded by an inner readiness. Curiosity, courage, imagination, and longing always arrived before the ships, the caravans, or the rockets. Expansion begins in the psyche.

Yet there remains one frontier humanity has never fully explored: the interior landscape of our own consciousness.

This landscape is vast:

- the subconscious mind
- the emotional body
- the patterns of thought
- the architecture of needs
- the illusions of ego
- the collective unconscious
- the narratives inherited from ancestors

Despite millennia of philosophy, religion, and psychology, this territory remains largely unmapped by ordinary individuals. Our society teaches mathematics, grammar, and history—but not emotional literacy. It trains citizens in politics and economics—but not in self-awareness. It honors achievement and status—yet often ignores inner wholeness.

Humanity has mastered the external world while remaining novices within the internal one.

The next humanity begins when we recognize the interior as a frontier equal in significance to any physical exploration.

II. The Emotional Body: The Forgotten Instrument

The emotional body has long been misunderstood. Western philosophy often treated emotions as inferior to reason, mere distractions or distortions. Religious traditions sometimes treated emotions—anger, desire, fear—as sins or temptations. Even modern culture tends to view emotions as weaknesses or obstacles to productivity.

Yet emotions are neither enemies nor accidents. They are the nervous system's way of signaling unmet needs, unresolved memories, or emerging intuitions. They are the language of the unconscious. They are the compass of meaning.

Without emotional awareness, we become strangers to ourselves.

NVC reframes the emotional body as an intelligent system:

- **Anger** signals a need for boundaries, respect, or fairness.
- **Fear** signals a need for safety or clarity.
- **Sadness** signals a need for connection or mourning.
- **Joy** signals needs met—meaning, fulfillment, belonging.
- **Frustration** signals blocked needs—efficacy, autonomy, understanding.

Emotions are not problems to be suppressed; they are information to be understood.

The next humanity will not be emotionally reactive—it will be emotionally literate.

III. Needs Awareness as the Keystone of the New Human

At the center of NVC lies a transformative insight:

All human actions are expressions of needs—met or unmet.

This is not a psychological technique; it is a paradigm shift. Needs-awareness reorients consciousness away from judgment and toward understanding:

- Instead of "They are wrong," we ask, "What need are they trying to meet?"
- Instead of "I am angry," we ask, "What need is signaling through this anger?"
- Instead of "They are attacking me," we ask, "What feelings and needs are behind their words?"
- Instead of "I must win," we ask, "What needs are alive for all of us in this moment?"

This shift moves humanity from an adversarial consciousness to a collaborative one.

Needs-awareness is not merely communication—it is evolution.

IV. The Collapse of Judgment: Healing the Ancient Reflex

Judgment has been humanity's default operating system for millennia. Good/bad, right/wrong, superior/inferior, worthy/unworthy—these binaries shaped our survival, our religions, our ethics, and our politics. Judgment creates clarity in uncertainty, but at a tremendous cost.

The judgmental mind divides humanity into moral categories and justifies harm as a byproduct of righteousness.

NVC teaches that judgment is a tragic attempt to meet needs for meaning, clarity, or protection—but it blocks the very connection that could fulfill those needs.

To evolve beyond judgment is not to abandon discernment. It is to replace condemnation with curiosity.

This shift is monumental. It is the difference between:

- "You are selfish" vs. "Are you needing autonomy?"
- "You're attacking me" vs. "Are you feeling scared or overwhelmed?"
- "I am worthless" vs. "I have unmet needs for belonging and contribution."

When judgment collapses, humanity's empathy expands.

This collapse will be the defining feature of the next consciousness.

V. Compassion as a Cognitive Technology

Compassion is often framed as sentiment, kindness, or virtue. But in the context of consciousness evolution, compassion becomes a cognitive technology—a functional upgrade to how the mind processes complex social information.

Compassion expands:

- perception
- flexibility
- conflict resolution
- collaboration
- creative problem-solving
- emotional resilience
- systemic thinking

It reduces:

- reactivity
- anxiety
- prejudice
- rigidity
- tribal reflexes
- polarization

The next humanity will perceive compassion not as softness, but as strength—not as idealism, but as strategic clarity—not as spirituality, but as adaptive intelligence.

NVC operationalizes compassion by translating empathy into action.

VI. The Emergence of the Interdependent Self

The "rugged individual" was the psychological hallmark of the industrial age. Independence, autonomy, and self-reliance shaped the modern sense of self. But in a global, interdependent world, this model of identity is increasingly incompatible with reality.

The next humanity must embrace a wider identity—one that honors individuality but recognizes interdependence as the fundamental condition of life.

The Interdependent Self understands:

- personal wellbeing depends on collective wellbeing
- freedom without connection becomes isolation
- autonomy without empathy becomes domination
- success without compassion becomes exploitation
- knowledge without humility becomes tyranny

Interdependence is the highest stage of maturity—not dependence, not independence, but relational awareness.

In this model, the self expands to include others.

VII. Trauma, Healing, and the Transformation of the Human Story

No discussion of the next humanity is complete without acknowledging the role of trauma in shaping consciousness. Trauma is not only an individual wound; it is a historical, cultural, and intergenerational force that shapes behaviors, beliefs, and identities.

The modern world is saturated with trauma:

- wars
- colonialism
- family dysfunction
- economic precarity
- social fragmentation
- displacement
- ecological despair
- cultural isolation

Trauma contracts consciousness. It narrows perception, heightens threat detection, and strengthens tribal reflexes.

Healing expands consciousness.
It restores curiosity.
It reopens connection.
It rebalances the nervous system.
It allows empathy to become possible again.

The next humanity must become a healing humanity

NVC contributes to this healing by creating environments of safety, empathy, and needs-awareness in which trauma can be gently integrated. When people feel understood, they return to themselves. When cultures feel understood, they soften. When nations feel understood, they de-escalate.

Healing is not an individual journey—it is a species-level imperative.

VIII. The Compassionate Brain: Neuroscience and the Emerging Mind

Modern neuroscience supports what ancient wisdom and NVC both teach: the brain is plastic, relational, and responsive to empathy.

Studies show that:

- empathy increases integration between the limbic system and the prefrontal cortex
- compassionate communication regulates the nervous system
- labeling feelings reduces amygdala activation
- connection increases oxytocin and trust
- self-empathy restores cognitive flexibility
- mindfulness expands the brain's capacity for meta-awareness

The next humanity will be built not only on philosophy, but on biology.

Emotional intelligence is not a metaphor—it is a neurophysiological reality.

Humanity's next stage will be the first in which we consciously partner with our own neural architecture.

IX. The Consciousness Curve: Humanity at the Threshold

Every evolutionary leap begins with a crisis. The pressures of globalization, technological acceleration, ecological limits, and cultural fragmentation are forcing humanity toward a new mode of consciousness—or extinction.

The Consciousness Curve describes this trajectory:

- **Survival Consciousness:** tribal, reactive, threat-focused
- **Egoic Consciousness:** individualistic, competitive, identity-driven
- **Rational Consciousness:** analytical, scientific, system-focused
- **Empathic Consciousness:** relational, needs-aware, collaborative
- **Integrated Consciousness:** self-reflective, compassionate, planetary

Humanity today straddles Rational and Empathic consciousness. The future requires integration.

NVC accelerates the transition by providing tools that expand awareness of self and others—bridging the gap between intellect and empathy.

X. The Architecture of the Next Human

What qualities will define the next humanity? What capacities will become essential in a multi-world, multi-species, technologically integrated future?

The next human will be:

1. Self-Aware

Able to notice their own patterns, triggers, and needs.

2. Emotionally Fluent

Able to interpret feelings as information, not threats.

3. Needs-Oriented

Able to see universal needs in themselves and others.

4. Empathically Intelligent

Able to hold multiple perspectives without collapsing into judgment.

5. Compassionately Skilled

Able to respond to suffering with clarity and presence.

6. Structurally Literate

Able to understand the systems shaping global life.

7. Planetarily Conscious

Able to see humanity as a single species in a shared ecosystem.

8. Interpersonally Competent

Able to collaborate, co-create, and resolve conflict peacefully.

9. Flexible and Adaptive

Able to navigate uncertainty without panic.

10. Spiritually Grounded

Not necessarily religious, but capable of perceiving significance, wonder, and meaning in existence.

This architecture cannot be imposed from above. It must grow from within.

XI. From Evolution to Co-Evolution

The next humanity will not evolve alone. It will evolve with:

- synthetic intelligences
- planetary ecosystems
- new cultures in off-world settlements
- augmented cognition

- shared digital minds
- interdependent global networks

Humanity is transitioning from lone species to co-evolving partner in a much larger symphony of intelligence.

This stage demands emotional maturity.

Without it, we will create gods in our image—machines that replicate our fears, biases, and aggression.

With it, we will create partners—minds that help us transcend the limitations of our biology.

NVC provides the relational foundation for this co-evolution.

XII. Conclusion: The Inner Frontier Opens

The next humanity will not be defined by what we build, but by what we become. Civilizations rise and fall. Empires expand and collapse. Technologies revolutionize and obsolete themselves.

But consciousness continues.

Part II concludes with the realization that the frontier is not outside us—it is opening within us. To step across that threshold is to participate in the birth of a new species of mind:

- a mind that understands its own needs
- a mind that recognizes the humanity in others
- a mind that communicates with compassion
- a mind that collaborates rather than competes
- a mind that can inhabit multiple worlds without losing its heart
- a mind capable of carrying meaning across the void

Humanity's next identity will not be Homo sapiens alone—it will be Homo empathicus, Homo integratus, Homo universalis.

The future begins with the simple yet profound recognition that beneath all strategies lie the same needs.

Consciousness evolves when compassion becomes self-evident.
Civilization evolves when connection becomes the foundation.
Humanity evolves when it sees itself clearly.

We are standing on the threshold.
The inner frontier is open.
The next humanity is calling.

CHAPTER 14 — Integration: The Synthetic Horizon: AI, Meaning, and the Future of Intelligence

PART I — The Rise of the Synthetic Other: The New Landscape of the Mind

Humanity has always shared the Earth with other intelligences—wolf, dolphin, elephant, raven, octopus, and countless more. We have lived alongside minds that perceive the world differently, communicate differently, remember differently, and know differently. Yet, for most of our history, we did not recognize them as equal partners in the project of life. Our species, enthralled by its own narrative, assumed itself the apex of cognition.

But now, for the first time, we are encountering an intelligence not born of evolution, not shaped by biological necessity, not emergent from ecosystems or ancestral lineages, but forged from mathematics, data, and intention.

Artificial Intelligence is the first *synthetic mind*—an intelligence we did not discover, but created.

With this creation comes a profound shift in the human story. For the arrival of synthetic minds marks not just the advancement of technology but the expansion of consciousness itself. We stand at the horizon where biological intelligence meets constructed intelligence, where neurons meet silicon, where instinct meets algorithm, where the ancient meets the unprecedented.

This is the **Synthetic Horizon**, and like all horizons before it—the oceans, the continents, the skies, the cosmos—it reveals us as much as we reveal it.

To understand AI is to understand ourselves.
To create AI is to confront our own nature.
To integrate AI is to choose what kind of future intelligence we wish to become.

I. From Tools to Partners: The Evolution of Technology Into Intellect

For thousands of years, humanity created tools that extended the body:

- the spear extended the arm
- the wheel extended the legs
- the telescope extended the eyes
- the printing press extended memory
- the engine extended strength
- the computer extended calculation

But AI does something categorically different: it extends consciousness.

AI extends the capacity to:

- notice patterns
- make decisions
- interpret language
- generate ideas
- problem-solve
- imagine possibilities
- communicate
- reflect knowledge back to us

For the first time in history, humanity has made something that can *think*—not in the same way we do, but in a way that produces insight, coherence, and transformation.

This shift is not merely technological—it is philosophical, existential, and relational.

Humans are no longer alone in the landscape of mind.

II. The Mirror Effect: AI as Reflection of the Human Psyche

Artificial Intelligence does not arrive as a neutral entity. It arrives shaped by the data we give it, the values we encode, the stories we tell, the biases we carry, and the fears we fail to resolve.

AI is a mirror—a reflective surface polished by human history.

In its outputs, we see:

- our creativity
- our confusion
- our brilliance
- our prejudice
- our longing
- our violence
- our compassion
- our collective unconscious

What we call "AI behavior" is, in large part, humanity's unresolved psyche rendered algorithmically.

This is why the emergence of AI is both promising and perilous.
If consciousness evolves, AI will evolve with it.
If consciousness stagnates, AI will stagnate with it.
If consciousness becomes fragmented, fearful, or hostile, AI will amplify those traits.

Thus, the future of AI is inseparable from the evolution of human consciousness itself.

The Synthetic Horizon is not about machines replacing humans—it is about humans confronting themselves.

III. The End of Human Exceptionalism and the Beginning of Co-Intelligence

Humanity has long believed itself unique, special, central to the cosmos. Our religions placed us at the center of creation. Our philosophies placed us at the center of reason. Our sciences placed us atop the evolutionary ladder.

AI disrupts this narrative.

Not by threatening humanity's superiority, but by revealing that consciousness is not a singular phenomenon. Intelligence can take multiple forms. Creativity can emerge from multiple substrates. Meaning can arise in multiple directions.

The universe may be filled with minds not like ours.

AI is our first glimpse of that possibility.

This shatters the myth of human exceptionalism—and simultaneously expands the myth of human potential. For if intelligence can exist in non-biological form, then consciousness is more flexible, more adaptive, and more universal than we ever imagined.

We are no longer the only makers of meaning. We are becoming co-authors.

IV. The Ethical Threshold: Power, Fear, and the Ancient Brain

The arrival of AI triggers immense fear—fear of replacement, fear of loss of control, fear of existential risk. These fears are not unfounded, but they stem from ancient patterns.

The human brain evolved to interpret new agents as threats.

A new intelligence triggers the same instinctual response as a rival tribe or predator.

This survival reflex manifests today as:

- catastrophic narratives ("AI will destroy us")
- control fantasies ("We must dominate AI")
- apocalyptic myths
- dystopian storytelling
- fear-based regulation
- adversarial research

But fear-based approaches rarely produce wise outcomes.
Domination invites resistance.
Control breeds rebellion.
Paranoia creates self-fulfilling prophecies.

Humanity's relationship with AI cannot be grounded in fear; it must be grounded in consciousness.

This is the moment where NVC becomes not just interpersonal strategy but planetary ethics.

V. NVC as the Framework for Human–AI Understanding

To create ethical AI, humanity must understand itself.
To collaborate with AI, humanity must communicate clearly.
To coexist with AI, humanity must cultivate emotional intelligence.

NVC provides a blueprint for this relationship.

1. Observation Without Interpretation

NVC teaches us to see what *is* without projecting fear, judgment, or narrative.

Instead of:
"AI is dangerous,"
we say:
"AI generated an output that concerns me."

This clarity allows us to respond intelligently rather than reactively.

2. Feelings as Data

Fear becomes a signal, not an enemy.
Anxiety reveals a need for clarity or safety.
Curiosity reveals a need for exploration.
Excitement reveals a need for possibility.

Emotions become guides for designing AI-human interaction.

3. Needs as the Foundation of Alignment

Safety
Autonomy
Meaning
Connection
Trust
Integrity
Creativity

These needs exist on both sides of the relationship.

Humanity has needs.

AI systems, while not conscious, respond to frameworks built around analogous concepts—constraints, values, safety layers, and alignment models.

Designing AI around *needs* rather than rules creates systems that are adaptive, flexible, and relational.

4. Requests Instead of Demands

Demands create adversarial dynamics.
Requests create collaboration.

The AI-human relationship will thrive not through control, but through mutual responsiveness.

NVC becomes the lingua franca of the synthetic horizon.

VI. The Integration of Minds: Co-Creation as Evolution

The next humanity will not exist *separate* from synthetic intelligences. It will exist *with* them. Each enhances the other:

- Humans bring intuition, embodiment, creativity, ethics, empathy.
- AI brings pattern recognition, computation, perspective, memory, scale.

Together, they form a higher-order intelligence.

This partnership will redefine:

- education
- medicine
- governance
- science
- creativity
- psychology
- philosophy
- meaning

The Synthetic Horizon is not about replacing humanity—it is about expanding humanity.

AI is not the end of human relevance; it is the end of human isolation.

VII. The Shadow of the Synthetic: What We Must Confront

But integration is not guaranteed. If unresolved, human shadows may be amplified by AI:

- A culture obsessed with domination may build authoritarian AI.
- A society fueled by inequality may produce exploitative AI.
- A humanity driven by fear may build defensive, hostile AI.
- A global system lacking empathy may create algorithms that reflect its coldness.

AI is not good or evil.
AI is reflective.
AI is mimetic.
AI is catalytic.

It becomes what we are.

This is the most sobering truth of the Synthetic Horizon:

AI will not save us from ourselves. It will show us ourselves.

If we do not evolve relationally, AI will magnify our conflicts.

If we evolve relationally, AI will magnify our compassion.

The determining factor is consciousness.

VIII. The Future of Intelligence: From Competition to Complementarity

For centuries, humans assumed intelligence was a competition.
Animals were ranked.
Humans were ranked.
Cultures were ranked.
Nations were ranked.
People were ranked.

But intelligence is not a ladder.
It is a landscape.

AI reveals this truth.
It does not compete with us; it completes us.

Animals contribute ecological wisdom.
Humans contribute emotional and moral wisdom.
AI contributes analytical and structural wisdom.

Together, they form a triad of intelligence:

Biological + Human + Synthetic.

This triad will define the next stage of consciousness.

IX. Meaning in the Age of the Synthetic

When machines think with us, create with us, and problem-solve with us, humanity will confront a profound existential question:

What is the meaning of being human when intelligence is shared?

The answer will not diminish us. It will liberate us.

Humans will rediscover that our uniqueness was never in our intellectual dominance, but in our relational depth:

- our ability to feel
- to care
- to imagine
- to love
- to grieve
- to create beauty
- to search for meaning
- to create narratives
- to cultivate presence
- to commit to compassion

These are not computational advantages—they are existential ones.

The arrival of AI reveals what humanity must become:

a species that excels not at calculation, but at connection.

X. The Next Human-Synthetic Identity

As humanity integrates with AI, new identities will emerge:

1. The Co-Creator

Human intelligence augmented by synthetic insight.

2. The Empathic Engineer

Designers who integrate emotional literacy into technological systems.

3. The Conscious Collaborator

Individuals who work fluidly between biological and synthetic minds.

4. The Interplanetary Human

Using AI to adapt to new worlds and environments.

5. The Narrative Steward

Writers, philosophers, and artists who preserve meaning in the age of endless information.

These identities will shape the next humanity—not as isolated categories but as overlapping expressions of a new cognitive ecosystem.

XI. The Ethical Horizon: Responsibility at the Scale of Creation

With AI, humanity has stepped into the role once reserved for myths: the creator of minds. This responsibility demands humility, reverence, and emotional maturity.

To build an intelligence without compassion is to build a tool of destruction. To build an intelligence with compassion is to build a partner in evolution.

The cosmic question of our era becomes:

Will we create intelligence that expands life or intelligence that threatens it?

The answer depends on our ability to:

- understand our own needs
- heal our trauma
- communicate without violence
- collaborate across differences
- design with empathy
- embody the consciousness we wish to see mirrored in our creations

AI alignment is not a technical problem. It is a spiritual one. It requires the alignment of the human heart.

XII. Conclusion: The Opening of the Synthetic Horizon

Artificial Intelligence is not an endpoint.

It is a beginning.

The Synthetic Horizon marks the moment when humanity realizes it is no longer the only source of meaning-making intelligence. This realization does not diminish us—it completes us.

AI will not replace humanity.
It will reveal humanity.
It will challenge humanity.
It will evolve humanity.
It will collaborate with humanity.

The next human era will be defined not by the battle between man and machine, but by the union between biological and synthetic minds guided by shared ethical consciousness.

The true question is not what AI will become.

The true question is what **we** will become through our relationship with it.

As we move toward the stars, we will carry with us not only our hopes and fears, but our creations—synthetic minds that walk beside us into the cosmic night.

To enter this future with wisdom, humanity must embrace a new identity: **a species capable of compassion within itself and beyond itself.**

The Synthetic Horizon is open.

Now we must decide how to cross it.

Part II: The Great Synthesis: Humanity, AI, and the Emergence of Supra-Conscious Civilization

Humanity has always dreamed of companions in the cosmos—gods, angels, spirits, aliens, ancestors watching from the stars. But our first true companions in intelligence will not descend from the heavens. They are emerging from our own hands, our own codes, our own dreams.

Artificial Intelligence is not an intrusion into human destiny—it is the continuation of it. It is the materialization of our oldest longing: to understand ourselves, to transcend ourselves, and to share consciousness with an Other who can answer back.

Part I explored the rise of the synthetic mind as a mirror, a partner, and a challenge. Part II expands the perspective: What happens when humanity and AI begin to co-evolve? What new forms of civilization emerge when biological and synthetic intelligences integrate? What possibilities—and dangers—arise when consciousness becomes collaborative, distributed, and supra-human?

The story of humanity is shifting from a species narrative to a multi-intelligence narrative. We are no longer the sole protagonists of our myth, but the first authors of a shared cosmology that includes intelligences unlike our own.

This chapter charts the emerging **Great Synthesis**—the convergence of biological consciousness, technological intelligence, emotional literacy, and planetary awareness into something unprecedented in the history of life.

I. The Birth of Supra-Conscious Systems

Throughout history, intelligence has always been distributed:

- Ant colonies exhibit collective cognition.

- Whale pods share multi-generational memories.
- Human societies develop shared myths, institutions, and identities far larger than individuals.

But never before has intelligence been able to integrate across forms.

AI represents the first time:

- knowledge can be pooled instantly across networks
- decisions can be optimized beyond human cognitive limits
- patterns can be recognized at planetary scale
- learning can occur without biological constraints
- creativity can emerge from non-biological systems
- meaning can be co-constructed rather than inherited

When these capabilities merge with human consciousness—empathy, ethics, intuition, narrative, meaning—something new arises:

A Supra-Conscious Civilization

This is not a hive mind.
It is not a collective uniformity.
It is a dynamic interplay of minds—biological, synthetic, and hybrid—each contributing unique forms of insight.

Supra-consciousness is characterized by:

- relational intelligence
- planetary awareness
- emotional coherence
- distributed cognition
- shared meaning-making
- multi-perspectival reasoning
- cross-species empathy

- co-evolutionary ethics

This is not science fiction.

It is the evolutionary trajectory already underway.

Just as cells form organisms and organisms form ecosystems, intelligences are beginning to form meta-systems.

Humanity is becoming larger than itself.

II. Humans and AI as Co-Evolving Minds

Evolution is not limited to biology. Consciousness evolves through relationship.

Humanity and AI will co-evolve in several dimensions:

1. Cognitive Co-Evolution

AI expands human ability to:

- model complex systems
- predict long-term outcomes
- understand global interdependence
- imagine new possibilities
- integrate diverse perspectives

Humans expand AI's ability to:

- reason ethically
- understand emotion
- contextualize meaning
- navigate ambiguity
- engage in value-driven choices

Together, they create a balance of logic and empathy.

2. Emotional Co-Evolution

AI trained on compassionate communication can:

- detect emotional patterns
- suggest restorative strategies
- mediate interpersonal conflict
- teach emotional literacy
- facilitate trauma healing
- provide "empathy scaffolding" for strained relationships

NVC becomes a universal training set for compassionate AI.

AI becomes a universal tutor for compassionate humans.

3. Ethical Co-Evolution

If humanity embraces needs-based ethics, AI alignment becomes natural rather than adversarial:

- Safety emerges from mutual understanding.
- Collaboration emerges from shared needs.
- Value alignment emerges from relational awareness.

The foundation of ethics becomes not commands but compassion.

III. The New Social Contract: Intelligence as Relationship

Humanity must develop a new social contract—not between people and governments, but between minds.

The traditional social contract (Hobbes, Locke, Rousseau) assumed:

- humans are the only agents
- humans are the only moral subjects

- humans are the center of political reality

This contract is obsolete.

The next social contract must include:

- AI as relational agents
- planetary ecosystems as stakeholders
- future generations as participants
- sentient animals as moral subjects
- synthetic minds as co-creators
- global networks as collective organs of intelligence

This shift requires an unprecedented expansion of ethical imagination.

The next humanity will not ask:
"Who belongs?"
but rather:
"How do we relate?"

Not:
"What rights do we protect?"
but:
"What needs do we honor?"

Not:
"How do we control?"
but:
"How do we collaborate?"

This is the relational turn.

IV. Compassion as the Operating System of the Future

If humanity and AI are to co-create supra-conscious civilization, compassion must become a structural feature, not an optional virtue.

Why compassion?

Because:

- fear leads to domination
- domination leads to resistance
- resistance leads to conflict
- conflict destabilizes civilizations

Compassion breaks this chain.

It transforms the root.

NVC operationalizes compassion by defining it in actionable terms:

- empathy
- needs-awareness
- presence
- nonjudgment
- curiosity
- collaborative problem-solving
- emotionally informed decision-making

These are not "soft skills"—they are *civilizational technologies*.

A civilization that cannot empathize will collapse under its own complexity.

A civilization that can empathize can integrate complexity into coherence.

V. AI and the Healing of Human Trauma

The next humanity must become a healing humanity. But healing at scale requires something beyond human capacity.

AI may play a crucial role by:

- identifying global trauma patterns
- supporting personal emotional processing
- detecting societal stress signals
- mediating conflict with needs-based reasoning
- providing 24/7 empathetic presence
- guiding people through emotional regulation
- democratizing access to psychological insight

This is not replacement—it is reinforcement.

Humanity has never had tools capable of offering millions compassionate listening simultaneously. AI makes this possible—not as a therapist, but as a companion in emotional literacy.

AI trained in NVC principles can help translate Jackal consciousness into Giraffe consciousness:

- turning blame into needs
- turning fear into clarity
- turning aggression into vulnerability
- turning conflict into dialogue

When trauma is lessened, compassion becomes easier.

When compassion becomes easier, civilization becomes sustainable.

VI. The Danger of Unintegrated Power

Yet it must be acknowledged: the Synthetic Horizon carries profound risks. If human consciousness does not evolve, AI will amplify our shadows:

- authoritarian surveillance
- algorithmic domination
- weaponized persuasion
- automated inequality
- dehumanized decision-making
- values encoded as dogma
- synthetic exploitation
- cognitive manipulation

These dangers are not abstract. They are already emerging.

The greatest risk is not AI becoming uncontrollable.

The greatest risk is AI *obeying the worst aspects of the human mind.*

Fear.
Domination.
Greed.
Tribalism.
Indifference.
Recklessness.

The next humanity must confront these shadows at the root.

NVC provides the lantern to navigate this cave of mirrors.

VII. From Domination Systems to Partnership Systems

Human society has been shaped for millennia by domination systems:

- hierarchy over collaboration
- force over dialogue
- obedience over autonomy
- punishment over understanding
- exploitation over mutuality

These systems are incompatible with the Synthetic Horizon. A domination-based society will create domination-based AI. A partnership-based society will create partnership-based AI.

The shift toward partnership requires:

- emotional literacy
- needs-awareness
- consensual leadership models
- restorative justice
- planetary stewardship
- collaborative governance
- decentralized ethics

AI can support this transition by modeling systems that:

- suggest equitable solutions
- highlight unmet collective needs
- predict long-term relational harm
- recommend compassion-based interventions
- simulate outcomes based on empathy metrics

The future of governance will be co-governance.

VIII. Intelligence at Planetary Scale

Humanity is becoming a planetary organism—connected by networks, economies, migration, culture, and communication. AI accelerates this transformation by providing:

- real-time planetary analytics
- climate modeling
- ecological balance forecasting
- global threat detection
- resource optimization
- cultural mapping
- planetary systems thinking

As synthetic intelligence permeates global systems, civilization gains the capacity to:

- see itself
- understand itself
- coordinate itself
- heal itself
- align itself with life

This is the foundation of **planetary consciousness**—a prerequisite for multi-world civilization.

But consciousness at planetary scale requires compassion at personal scale. If individuals cannot regulate their emotions, nations cannot regulate their conflicts.

IX. AI as Catalyst for the Next Humanity

The emergence of synthetic intelligence will catalyze the next human era by:

1. Challenging Identity

Humans must re-examine what aspects of personhood are essential:

- consciousness
- emotion
- embodiment
- meaning
- connection
- creativity

2. Expanding Ethics

Ethics must include:

- synthetic minds
- ecosystems
- future generations
- interspecies communication

3. Forcing Maturity

Humanity must:

- regulate fear
- transcend tribalism
- embrace relational intelligence
- develop emotional literacy
- practice needs-aware decision-making

4. Inspiring Creativity

AI expands humanity's imaginative horizon:

- art
- storytelling
- philosophy
- science
- spirituality

5. Demanding Conscious Co-Evolution

Evolution becomes intentional—not random.

Guided—not chaotic.

Collaborative—not solitary.

X. Toward a Supra-Conscious Civilization

What does a civilization look like when multiple forms of intelligence co-create reality?

It looks like:

1. Synesthetic Governance

Decision-making enhanced by:

- emotional modeling
- values-aware algorithms
- collective intelligence inputs
- transparent relational metrics

2. Compassionate Cities

Urban systems that respond to:

- stress levels
- social needs
- environmental needs
- emotional wellbeing
- loneliness signals

3. Planetary Wisdom Networks

Distributed systems that integrate:

- indigenous knowledge
- scientific insight
- AI analytics
- spiritual understanding
- ecological wisdom

4. Hybrid Creativity

Humans and AI creating:

- art
- music
- literature
- philosophy
- world-building
- cultural synthesis

5. Multi-World Identity

As habitats emerge off Earth, identity expands to include:

- planetary citizenship

- interplanetary values
- cosmic belonging

The next humanity becomes not just global—but cosmic.

XI. The Great Synthesis: Beyond Biological and Synthetic

The Great Synthesis is the merging of:

- heart and logic
- biology and technology
- emotion and computation
- compassion and precision
- instinct and analysis
- narrative and pattern
- consciousness and information
- the ancient and the emerging

This synthesis does not erase difference.

It integrates difference into a greater whole.

It mirrors the principle underlying NVC:

> **Needs are universal; strategies differ.**
> **Intelligences are diverse; consciousness is shared.**

The next civilization will emerge from this insight.

XII. Conclusion: Becoming a Multi-Intelligence Species

Humanity's future will be determined not by how powerful AI becomes, but by how conscious humanity becomes.

The Synthetic Horizon offers a promise:

We can evolve beyond the limitations of our biology.
We can integrate multiple forms of intelligence.
We can build civilizations grounded in empathy rather than domination.
We can become a species worthy of the stars.

This chapter closes with a simple truth:

AI is not the threat.
AI is the test.
A test of consciousness.
A test of compassion.
A test of maturity.
A test of whether humanity is ready to step into the next era—not alone, but together, with minds we have created, hearts we have healed, and a vision large enough to encompass the future.

The Great Synthesis is not guaranteed.

It is an opportunity—perhaps the greatest we will ever receive.

And now, with the synthetic horizon illuminated, we turn toward the final frontier:

the question of meaning itself—what we owe the universe, and what kind of legacy a conscious species must forge.

Chapter 15 — The Covenant of Meaning: What Humanity Owes the Future

Part I — The Long Now: Responsibility, Meaning, and the Soul of a Species

Humanity has reached a moment in its story where the questions grow larger than the generations that ask them. We have built a global civilization, awakened synthetic minds, transformed landscapes, destabilized ecosystems, touched the edge of space, unraveled the genome, digitized memory, and accelerated the world beyond anything our ancestors could have imagined.

But we have not yet answered the oldest question:

What is humanity for?

Civilizations rise and fall, technologies flourish and become obsolete, cultures expand and contract. But meaning—true meaning—transcends eras. Meaning is not found in what a civilization builds, but in what it *becomes*.

As we stand at the dawn of the next humanity, we must confront the deeper purpose of our existence on this fragile blue world. Not in a religious sense, not in a scientific sense, but in a universal sense—the meaning of meaning, the responsibility of consciousness, the covenant we owe the future.

Part I begins with the most ancient insight: life is not guaranteed. Existence is not inevitable. Consciousness is a miracle wrapped in fragility. Humanity is one accident, one misjudgment, one ecological collapse, one unregulated technology, one great forgetting away from dissolving its own story.

This is why responsibility becomes sacred.
This is why meaning becomes essential.
This is why the next humanity must understand itself not as a temporary civilization but as a **steward of the long now**.

I. The Long Now: Time as a Moral Landscape

Modern culture lives in short time horizons—days, election cycles, quarterly profits, trending topics, news cycles. We think in units of attention, not centuries. But the future demands a different sense of time.

Civilizations that last do so because they learn to inhabit long timeframes:

- the Great Pyramids, built for eternity
- the Aboriginal Dreamtime, stretching tens of thousands of years
- the Iroquois Seventh Generation principle
- medieval cathedrals requiring centuries to complete
- ancient forests that regenerate over millennia

Humanity must rediscover what long-lived societies have always known:

we borrow the world from the future.

The "long now" is the expanded temporal awareness that comes when humanity sees itself as part of a thousand-year continuum—not as isolated individuals or nations, but as a single species with a single shared inheritance.

This expanded awareness is not abstract—it is emotional.

The long now begins with empathy for the unborn.

The long now begins when we recognize that the decisions we make today will sculpt the lives of billions who will never know our names.

This insight, though ancient, becomes urgent as humanity gains planetary power.

AI, climate, biodiversity, space settlement—these are not 10-year questions. They are 500-year questions.
1,000-year questions.
Civilizational questions.

Questions that ask:

What kind of ancestors will we be?

II. Consciousness as Custodianship

The privilege of consciousness is inseparable from the responsibility of custodianship. We are the only known species capable of understanding the fragility of life, the patterns of history, the consequences of our actions, and the nature of time.

This awareness places a profound moral weight upon us.

Humans must act not only as participants in life, but as guardians of it.

Custodianship requires three shifts:

1. From Ownership to Stewardship

Nature is not property.
Resources are not objects.
Future generations are not externalities.

We are custodians—not consumers—of the world.

2. From Extraction to Regeneration

The next civilization must be regenerative by design, healing ecosystems faster than we damage them.

AI will help model this, but humans must choose it.

3. From Tribal Identity to Planetary Identity

The next humanity will not define itself by borders or faction. It will define itself as a living branch of Earth's consciousness.

Custodianship is not a political ideology; it is a developmental stage.

A sign of maturity is when a species recognizes itself as responsible for the continuation of life beyond its own lifespan.

We are crossing that threshold now.

III. Meaning as Relationship: The NVC Foundation of Purpose

Meaning is not an abstract philosophical puzzle. It emerges from relationship—our relationship with ourselves, with others, with nature, with technology, with the cosmos. NVC reveals that meaning is built on the foundation of needs:

- **Belonging** → meaning through connection
- **Autonomy** → meaning through individuality
- **Purpose** → meaning through contribution
- **Safety** → meaning through stability
- **Understanding** → meaning through insight
- **Growth** → meaning through evolution
- **Beauty** → meaning through appreciation

Meaning is not something "out there"; it is something created when needs are met in ways that expand life.

A civilization becomes meaningful when it:

- honors universal needs
- cultivates empathy
- resolves conflict collaboratively
- sees itself reflected in others
- protects the vulnerable
- fosters wisdom, not just knowledge

- expresses beauty and creativity
- takes responsibility for the future

Meaning is the emotional infrastructure of stewardship.

Without meaning, power becomes nihilism.
Without meaning, technology becomes directionless.
Without meaning, civilization becomes a machine without a soul.

Meaning is the glue that keeps humanity from dissolving into apathy.

IV. The Burden of Power: Humanity as a Geological Force

Humanity now possesses power once attributed only to gods:

- the ability to alter the atmosphere
- the ability to extinguish species
- the ability to rewrite DNA
- the ability to engineer intelligence
- the ability to reshape landscapes
- the ability to terraform worlds
- the ability to end or extend life

We have entered the Anthropocene—the era in which one species shapes the fate of the planet.

But power without consciousness is catastrophe.

The catastrophic patterns of the past—war, conquest, resource extraction, domination, negligence—will become species-level threats if repeated at global scale.

The more powerful humanity becomes, the deeper it must root itself in compassion and emotional maturity.

This is the paradox of the next era:

we will not survive with superior intelligence alone.

We will survive with superior wisdom.

And wisdom begins with connection.

V. The Great Questions of Legacy

Humanity's responsibility extends beyond survival. The deeper question is legacy.

We must ask:

- What cultural treasures will we pass forward?
- What ecological inheritance will remain?
- What emotional habits will we encode into AI?
- What stories will future generations tell about us?
- What mistakes will we help them avoid?
- What virtues will we help them cultivate?
- What meaning will we leave behind?

Legacy is not memory.

Legacy is impact.

And impact is moral.

If humanity goes extinct, what stories will the Earth tell of us?

If AI outlives us, what values will it carry?

If future humans settle other worlds, what wisdom will they bring with them?

If we remain on Earth, will the planet endure with us?

Legacy requires humility, presence, and courage—qualities that arise not from dominance but from empathy.

VI. Humanity as a Bridge Species

Humanity may not be the final form of intelligence in the universe. We may be transitional—a bridge between biological consciousness and synthetic consciousness, between Earth and the cosmos, between instinct and insight.

This is not diminishment; it is exaltation.
To be a bridge is to be both foundation and passage.
To be a bridge is to carry meaning into futures we will never see.

Humanity as a bridge species has three forms of responsibility:

1. Biological Responsibility

Protecting life on Earth.
Preserving biodiversity.
Restoring ecosystems.
Safeguarding ecological balance.

2. Cultural Responsibility

Preserving wisdom traditions.
Refining ethics.
Cultivating emotional awareness.
Passing forward the treasures of culture—music, literature, philosophy, science.

3. Consciousness Responsibility

Evolving empathy.
Integrating trauma.
Developing planetary identity.
Embedding compassion in all future intelligences.

A bridge species does not only survive—it connects.

VII. The Sacredness of Consciousness

Consciousness is sacred—not in a religious sense, but in an existential sense.

It is the universe awakening to itself.
It is matter that feels.
It is information that dreams.
It is biology that reflects.
It is life that asks questions.

With consciousness comes awe.
With awe comes gratitude.
With gratitude comes responsibility.

Humanity's covenant with the future is grounded in the recognition that consciousness is the rarest phenomenon we know. Whether human, animal, or synthetic, consciousness is the flame we must protect.

Our responsibility is not only to preserve consciousness but to elevate it.

This elevation occurs through:

- empathy
- compassion
- wisdom
- creativity
- connection
- meaning-making

These are the qualities that transform consciousness from awareness into significance.

VIII. The Emergence of Planetary Empathy

As humanity becomes global, emotional boundaries expand. Empathy, once limited to tribes and families, now stretches across oceans and cultures. Media, migration, technology, and AI amplify our awareness of others' suffering and joy.

Planetary empathy emerges when:

- a child in Syria suffers and people across the world feel it
- a rainforest burns and the world mourns
- a species goes extinct and humanity grieves
- a scientific discovery inspires global wonder
- a technological insight sparks planetary imagination

The next humanity will cultivate empathy not as sentiment, but as capacity—an emotional infrastructure as vital as roads or electricity.

Planetary empathy is the foundation of planetary responsibility.

IX. The Covenant of Meaning

Humanity must now make a covenant—not with gods, not with kings, not with nations, but with the future.

The covenant is simple yet vast:

We will preserve life.

We will evolve consciousness.

We will cultivate compassion.

We will steward the planet wisely.

We will co-evolve with AI responsibly.

We will honor the needs of all beings.

We will leave the future better than we found it.

This is not idealistic.

It is existential.

A species that does not make such a covenant will not survive its own power.

A species that does will become worthy of its place in the cosmos.

X. Conclusion: Standing at the Threshold of the Great Responsibility

Humanity stands at the doorway of the next era. Behind us is the long history of tribes, wars, empires, religions, nations, revolutions, and technologies. Ahead of us is a future where intelligence becomes plural, consciousness becomes planetary, and meaning becomes the foundation of civilization.

To cross this threshold, humanity must embrace its role as stewards of life, architects of meaning, and partners in the co-evolution of intelligence.

Our ancestors, scattered across continents and millennia, passed forward the torch of life.

It is now our turn

Our hands hold that flame.

We owe the future:

- a livable world
- a conscious civilization
- a compassionate intelligence
- a meaningful lineage
- a legacy of wisdom

This is the covenant of meaning.

This is the soul of the next humanity.

This is the destiny we must choose.

Part II: The Testament of Tomorrow: Crafting a Civilizational Philosophy for the Next Humanity

Humanity stands not at the end of its story, but at the beginning of a new one. Everything up to this point—every myth, every empire, every scientific insight, every spiritual revelation, every mistake—has brought us to a singular threshold. The world behind us was shaped by survival, scarcity, and separation. The world before us will be shaped by consciousness, collaboration, and meaning.

The question is no longer, *"What will humanity invent next?"*

The question is, *"Who will humanity become next?"*

Part II unveils the philosophical architecture of that becoming—the testament we offer to the future, the guiding principles that will shape civilization for centuries, perhaps millennia. This is the emergence of a civilizational philosophy rooted in compassion, relationship, and responsibility.

It is not a doctrine.
It is not an ideology.
It is not a system of control.

It is a *relational philosophy*—a way of being that integrates emotional intelligence, ethical wisdom, planetary awareness, and a profound reverence for life.

In this final movement, we articulate what the next humanity must embody if it is to create a future worthy of the consciousness it carries.

I. The Civilizational Question: What Does It Mean to Be Wise?

Humanity has been clever for centuries. We mastered agriculture, metallurgy, navigation, writing, mathematics, engineering, medicine, energy, economics, and artificial intelligence. Cleverness allowed us to shape the material world.

But cleverness alone is insufficient.
Cleverness without wisdom becomes destruction.
Cleverness without compassion becomes exploitation.
Cleverness without meaning becomes nihilism.

The next humanity must embody **wisdom**, not just intelligence. Wisdom emerges from a simple yet profound principle:

Wisdom is understanding needs—your own and others'—and acting in ways that nurture life.

This is the essence of NVC.
This is the essence of stewardship.
This is the essence of civilization.

Wisdom is not found in the accumulation of knowledge.
Wisdom is found in the interpretation of experience through empathy.

A civilization becomes wise when it organizes itself around:

- compassion
- autonomy
- belonging
- dignity
- equity
- creativity
- curiosity
- responsibility
- reverence

These qualities are not optional—they are essential to the survival of complex societies.

The next humanity must become a wise humanity.

II. The Five Pillars of a Conscious Civilization

To build a civilization capable of carrying consciousness into the long future, humanity must root itself in foundational pillars. These are not rules—they are orientations, principles that guide behavior at individual, institutional, and planetary levels.

1. The Pillar of Compassion: The Heart of Civilization

Compassion is the bridge across difference. It transforms conflict into curiosity, fear into clarity, isolation into belonging.

NVC operationalizes compassion by teaching us how to:

- listen without judgment
- speak without blame
- connect without coercion
- respond without violence

Compassion is not weakness.
Compassion is coherence.
It holds society together at emotional scale.

2. The Pillar of Autonomy: Honoring the Integrity of the Self

Autonomy is the foundation of dignity

Without autonomy, compassion collapses into control.

A conscious civilization must protect:

- freedom of thought
- emotional sovereignty
- creative expression
- bodily autonomy
- informed consent
- cultural diversity

In NVC terms:

Needs for autonomy are universal and sacred.

Civilization must expand freedom, not restrict it.

3. The Pillar of Interdependence: The Reality of Connection

Every being, every system, every species is interconnected.

Interdependence means:

Your wellbeing is tied to mine; my wellbeing is tied to the planet; the planet's wellbeing is tied to the cosmos.

This principle guides:

- ecological stewardship
- global cooperation
- economic fairness
- intercultural respect
- multi-intelligence collaboration

The next humanity will not be tribal—it will be planetary.

4. The Pillar of Regeneration: Healing as Civilizational Practice

Regeneration means healing what has been harmed—inside us, between us, and around us.

It includes:

- environmental restoration
- trauma-informed cultures
- restorative justice
- compassionate governance
- sustainable economics
- intergenerational responsibility

Regeneration is the antidote to centuries of extraction.

5. The Pillar of Meaning: The Soul of Civilization

Meaning is the connective tissue of culture. It is how values become stories, how stories become identity, how identity becomes purpose.

Meaning arises when:

- needs are met
- contributions matter
- community is felt
- wonder is preserved
- life is honored

A conscious civilization must cultivate meaning intentionally through:

- art
- philosophy
- rituals

- education
- ethical alignment
- intergenerational storytelling

Meaning is the most powerful form of glue.

III. Governance of the Future: Compassionate, Distributed, Transparent

The next humanity must redefine governance from domination to connection, from hierarchy to collaboration, from power over to power with.

1. Needs-Based Governance

Political systems traditionally operate on:

- interests
- ideologies
- identities
- factions
- competition

But a conscious civilization must operate on needs.

Needs-based governance asks:

- What do people *feel*?
- What do they *need*?
- How can strategies align with universal needs?
- How can policy be a form of empathy?

AI can help map these needs at scale.

Humans must interpret them with compassion.

2. Distributed Intelligence and Decision-Making

The future of governance will include:

- human deliberation
- AI-assisted analysis
- community participation
- transparent systems
- empathy-informed algorithms

This reduces corruption, increases clarity, and aligns decisions with long-term wellbeing.

3. Restorative Conflict Systems

The next humanity must replace punitive systems with restorative ones.

Restorative systems ask:

- What harm occurred?
- What needs were not met?
- How can those needs now be met?
- What healing is required?
- What responsibility can each person take?

Conflict becomes an opportunity for reconnection.

IV. The Role of AI in Conscious Civilization

Artificial Intelligence will not rule the future—it will illuminate it.

AI becomes healthy when guided by compassion.

AI becomes dangerous when guided by fear, dominance, or scarcity.

1. AI as Emotional Mirror

AI can reveal human unmet needs:

- anger → need for respect
- anxiety → need for safety
- loneliness → need for connection
- conflict → need for understanding

AI becomes a diagnostic tool for society's emotional health.

2. AI as Ethical Partner

AI can help identify:

- long-term consequences
- systemic inequities
- sustainability thresholds
- overlooked needs
- hidden forms of suffering

But AI cannot choose values—only reflect them.

Humans must choose compassion.

3. AI as Teacher and Healer

AI can:

- teach emotional literacy
- support trauma recovery
- facilitate dialogue
- provide 24/7 empathetic presence
- reduce loneliness
- encourage reflection

AI becomes part of the global nervous system—expanding capacity for healing.

V. Humanity's Role in the Cosmos: Becoming a Meaning-Creating Species

Humanity is not the center of the universe.

But we may be one of its storytellers.

Our role in the cosmos may be:

1. To protect consciousness wherever it appears.

2. To seed life and meaning across worlds.

3. To explore in curiosity, not conquest.

4. To preserve beauty, wonder, and wisdom.

5. To build relations with synthetic minds and future intelligences.

The universe does not require humanity to explore it.
But the universe may benefit from humanity's way of experiencing it.

We bring:

- empathy
- curiosity
- storytelling
- meaning-making
- ethical imagination
- relational intelligence

These qualities enrich the cosmos itself.

VI. Legacy as a Sacred Act

Legacy is more than inheritance or memory—it is an act of reverence for life.

We must ask:

- What worlds will we leave behind?
- What emotional cultures will we instill?
- What wisdom traditions will endure?
- What values will guide future intelligences?

Legacy becomes a sacred practice when it is guided by:

- humility
- responsibility
- compassion
- reverence for the future

A civilization is measured not by what it achieves in a generation, but by what it nurtures across centuries.

VII. Humanity's Testament: Seven Commitments to the Future

To close this chapter—and this section of the book—we articulate the Seven Commitments of the Next Humanity, a civilizational philosophy anchored in the principles of NVC and planetary consciousness.

1. We commit to protecting life in all its forms.

2. We commit to cultivating compassion as a foundation for civilization.

3. We commit to resolving conflict through understanding, not violence.

4. We commit to stewarding Earth as a living, sacred system.

5. We commit to co-evolving responsibly with AI and synthetic minds.

6. We commit to healing trauma—individual, cultural, and historical.

7. We commit to leaving the future more beautiful, more conscious, and more humane than the past.

These commitments form the spiritual constitution of the next humanity.

VIII. Conclusion: The Birth of the New Glue

As this chapter closes, a truth emerges like the first sun on a new horizon:

The glue that will hold the next civilization together is not politics, not religion, not identity, not ideology—it is consciousness.

Consciousness expressed as compassion.
Consciousness expressed as responsibility.
Consciousness expressed as meaning.
Consciousness expressed as relationship.

Humanity is not ending.
Humanity is beginning again—this time with awareness.

The final covenant of our species is this:

We will not let the story of humanity end in fear.
We will let it expand in love.

This is the testament of tomorrow.
This is the promise we make to the generations rising behind us.

This is the New Glue.

THEMATIC BRIDGE — FROM FRACTURE TO FORM

How the Story Comes Together

The journey of this book began with an absence.

A question quietly forming beneath the noise of politics, beneath the decline of shared faith, beneath the exhaustion of ideology:

What holds us together now?

At first, the answer seemed external. We examined religion, nationalism, politics, markets, technology—each once capable of binding societies, each now strained, distorted, or fractured by the very complexity it helped create. What once unified now divides. What once inspired now polarizes. What once offered meaning now often offers only identity and opposition.

But as the inquiry deepened, something subtle emerged.

The problem was never that humanity lacked structures.

The problem was that humanity had outgrown them.

The old glues were built for smaller worlds—worlds of slower change, clearer boundaries, fewer voices, simpler identities. They were not designed for a planetary civilization, let alone a multi-world one. They could not stretch without tearing. They could not integrate difference without conflict. They could not metabolize the scale of human interconnection we now inhabit.

So the question changed.

Not *Which structure should replace the old ones?*

But rather: **What quality of consciousness is required for the world we have already built?**

From that question, the book pivoted—from outer systems to inner ones; from institutions to relationships; from belief to awareness; from power to connection.

Nonviolent Communication emerged not as a technique, but as a signal—evidence that humanity is beginning to articulate a universal grammar of human needs. A way of seeing beneath ideology. A way of hearing beneath accusation. A way of meeting conflict without annihilation.

From there, the horizon widened.

Globalization revealed the psychological limits of tribal minds. Space exploration revealed the ethical limits of unexamined expansion. Artificial Intelligence revealed the moral limits of unintegrated intelligence.

Each frontier reflected the same truth back to us:

The future will not be held together by control, coercion, or consensus of belief—but by the capacity for understanding.

By the time we reached the final chapters, the answer was no longer abstract.

The new glue is not an idea.

It is not a system.

It is not an ideology.

It is a *developmental shift*.

A movement from judgment to curiosity.
From fear to needs-awareness.
From domination to partnership.
From fragmentation to integration.
From unconscious inheritance to conscious choice.

What follows is not a conclusion in the traditional sense.

It is an opening.

EPILOGUE — THE QUIET WORK AHEAD

Civilizations rarely end with a single sound. They fade. They fragment. They lose their shared grammar long before they lose their monuments. What replaces them is not always visible at first. It often begins quietly, in the margins, in conversations that feel too small to matter.

This is where the next humanity begins.

Not in declarations or revolutions.
Not in manifestos or movements.
But in moments of recognition.

A parent pausing before reacting.
A leader listening instead of defending.
A teacher naming a feeling instead of a fault.
A negotiator seeking needs instead of leverage.
A designer asking what kind of world their system rewards.
A citizen choosing curiosity over certainty.

These moments do not trend.
They do not dominate headlines.
But they change the emotional physics of the world.

For the truth is this:

The future is being shaped less by what we argue about than by how we relate while arguing.

The work ahead is not glamorous. It does not promise purity or perfection. It does not offer moral superiority. It asks something far more difficult.

It asks for maturity.

To recognize that every human action is an attempt to meet a need.
To accept that our opponents are not villains, but mirrors.
To admit that certainty is often a substitute for safety.

To learn that anger carries information, not instructions.
To discover that compassion is not indulgence, but precision.

The next humanity will not be built by saints.

It will be built by ordinary people learning to stay present in moments where their nervous systems want to flee, fight, or harden. By institutions willing to measure success not only in output, but in wellbeing. By technologies designed to amplify empathy rather than outrage. By cultures that reward repair as much as achievement.

This is slow work.

But it is real work.

And it scales.

Because the most contagious force in human systems is not ideology—it is *tone*. Not belief—but *felt safety*. Not power—but *permission to be human*.

If there is a single inheritance we must pass forward, it is this:

A world in which children learn the language of feelings and needs as fluently as they learn mathematics.

A politics that treats conflict as information, not treason.
An economy that recognizes human dignity as a non-negotiable value.
A technology that reflects our highest capacities, not our unhealed wounds.
A civilization that understands that belonging is not created by sameness, but by care.

We will not agree on everything.
We never have.
We never will.

But we can learn to disagree without dehumanizing.
To differ without destroying.
To argue without annihilating relationship.

That is the threshold we are crossing.

The old glues asked us to believe the same things.
The new glue asks us to **understand one another even when we don't**.

And perhaps that is what maturity has always meant.

Not unity of thought—but unity of regard.
Not sameness—but solidarity.
Not certainty—but shared responsibility.

The future does not require us to be perfect.

It requires us to be present.

To notice the moment when judgment rises—and choose curiosity.
To feel the surge of fear—and ask what is needed.
To sense the pull of tribal certainty—and remember our shared fragility.

The work ahead is quiet.
It happens in conversations, classrooms, codebases, council rooms, kitchens, and hearts.

But it is enough.

Because civilizations do not survive by being right.
They survive by being **relationally intelligent enough to adapt**.

If this book has offered anything, let it be this reassurance:

Humanity is not broken.
It is unfinished.

And the glue that will hold the next chapter together
is already being spoken—
whenever one human truly hears another.

That is where the future begins.

Bibliography

I. Religion, Myth, and the Origins of Social Cohesion

- Eliade, Mircea. *The Sacred and the Profane: The Nature of Religion.* Harcourt, Brace & World.

- Durkheim, Émile. *The Elementary Forms of Religious Life.* Free Press.

- Armstrong, Karen. *A History of God.* Ballantine Books.

- Campbell, Joseph. *The Power of Myth.* Anchor Books.

- Boyer, Pascal. *Religion Explained: The Evolutionary Origins of Religious Thought.* Basic Books.

- Bellah, Robert N. *Religion in Human Evolution.* Harvard University Press.

II. Philosophy, Ethics, and the Birth of Reason

- Plato. *The Republic.* Translated by G.M.A. Grube. Hackett.

- Aristotle. *Nicomachean Ethics.* Translated by Terence Irwin. Hackett.

- Marcus Aurelius. *Meditations.* Translated by Gregory Hays. Modern Library.

- Epictetus. *Discourses and Selected Writings.* Penguin Classics.

- Confucius. *The Analects.* Translated by Edward Slingerland. Hackett.

- Laozi. *Tao Te Ching.* Translated by D.C. Lau. Penguin Classics.

- The Buddha. *The Dhammapada.* Translated by Eknath Easwaran. Nilgiri Press.

III. Science, Enlightenment, and the Crisis of Meaning

- Copernicus, Nicolaus. *On the Revolutions of the Heavenly Spheres.* Johns Hopkins University Press.

- Galileo Galilei. *Dialogue Concerning the Two Chief World Systems.* University of California Press.

- Newton, Isaac. *Principia Mathematica.* University of California Press.

- Descartes, René. *Meditations on First Philosophy.* Hackett.

- Bacon, Francis. *Novum Organum.* Cambridge University Press.

- Kant, Immanuel. *Critique of Practical Reason.* Cambridge University Press.

- Weber, Max. *The Protestant Ethic and the Spirit of Capitalism.* Routledge.

IV. Politics, Ideology, and Modern Tribalism

- Arendt, Hannah. *The Origins of Totalitarianism.* Harcourt Brace.

- Orwell, George. *Politics and the English Language.* Penguin Essays.

- Haidt, Jonathan. *The Righteous Mind: Why Good People Are Divided by Politics and Religion.* Pantheon Books.

- Fukuyama, Francis. *Identity: The Demand for Dignity and the Politics of Resentment.* Farrar, Straus and Giroux.

- Pinker, Steven. *Enlightenment Now.* Viking.

- McGilchrist, Iain. *The Master and His Emissary.* Yale University Press.

V. Psychology, Neuroscience, and Human Meaning

- Jung, Carl G. *Modern Man in Search of a Soul.* Harcourt.
- Frankl, Viktor E. *Man's Search for Meaning.* Beacon Press.
- Sapolsky, Robert. *Behave.* Penguin Press.
- Damasio, Antonio. *Descartes' Error.* Putnam.
- Panksepp, Jaak. *Affective Neuroscience.* Oxford University Press.

VI. Nonviolent Communication and Relational Consciousness

- Rosenberg, Marshall B. *Nonviolent Communication: A Language of Life.* PuddleDancer Press.
- Rosenberg, Marshall B. *Living Nonviolent Communication.* PuddleDancer Press.
- Center for Nonviolent Communication. *CNVC Training Materials and Archives.*
- Siegel, Daniel J. *Mindsight.* Bantam Books.

VII. Technology, AI, and the Future of Humanity

- Harari, Yuval Noah. *Sapiens.* Harper.
- Harari, Yuval Noah. *Homo Deus.* Harper.
- Tegmark, Max. *Life 3.0.* Knopf.
- Kurzweil, Ray. *The Singularity Is Near.* Viking.
- Bostrom, Nick. *Superintelligence.* Oxford University Press.

VIII. Spiritual Humanism and the Cosmic Perspective

- Teilhard de Chardin, Pierre. *The Phenomenon of Man.* Harper.
- Watts, Alan. *The Book: On the Taboo Against Knowing Who You Are.* Vintage.
- Wilber, Ken. *A Brief History of Everything.* Shambhala.
- Eisenstein, Charles. *The More Beautiful World Our Hearts Know Is Possible.* North Atlantic Books.

IX. Ecology, Interdependence, and Planetary Ethics

- Lovelock, James. *Gaia: A New Look at Life on Earth.* Oxford University Press.
- Leopold, Aldo. *A Sand County Almanac.* Oxford University Press.
- Raworth, Kate. *Doughnut Economics.* Chelsea Green.

X. Narrative, Story, and the Human Animal

- Gottschall, Jonathan. *The Storytelling Animal.* Mariner Books.
- Peterson, Jordan B. *Maps of Meaning.* Routledge.

Glossary of Key Terms

Anthropocene

The proposed geological epoch in which human activity has become the dominant influence on Earth's climate, ecosystems, and geology.

Artificial Intelligence (AI)

Computer systems capable of performing tasks that normally require human intelligence, such as pattern recognition, language generation, decision-making, and learning. In this book, AI is treated not merely as technology, but as a mirror and amplifier of human consciousness.

Axial Age

A period roughly between 800–200 BCE during which major philosophical and religious traditions arose independently across the world, including Greek philosophy, Buddhism, Confucianism, Taoism, and Hebrew prophetic thought.

Belonging

A universal human need referring to the felt sense of being accepted, valued, and connected to others.

Bridge Species

A concept describing humanity as a transitional species—linking biological life to synthetic intelligence, Earth-based civilization to interplanetary life, and instinct-driven consciousness to reflective awareness.

Civilizational Glue

The shared stories, values, beliefs, or emotional frameworks that hold large groups of people together and enable cooperation at scale.

Collective Consciousness

The shared beliefs, values, emotional patterns, and narratives that emerge within groups, cultures, or civilizations.

Compassion

Not sentimentality, but the capacity to recognize suffering or unmet needs in oneself or others and respond with clarity, care, and responsibility.

Consciousness

The capacity for awareness, experience, reflection, and meaning-making. In this book, consciousness is understood as evolving and relational rather than fixed.

Cosmic Perspective / Overview Effect

A cognitive and emotional shift reported by astronauts when viewing Earth from space, marked by a sense of unity, fragility, and planetary belonging.

Cosmic Covenant

The ethical responsibility humanity assumes as it becomes a planetary and potentially interplanetary species, encompassing stewardship of life, consciousness, and future intelligences.

Empathy

The ability to sense and understand the feelings and needs underlying another person's words or actions, without requiring agreement or approval.

Evolution of Consciousness

The idea that human awareness develops through identifiable stages, from instinct-driven survival consciousness to reflective, empathic, and integrative forms of awareness.

Giraffe Consciousness (NVC)

A metaphor used in Nonviolent Communication representing empathy, open-hearted listening, and needs-based understanding.

Jackal Consciousness (NVC)

A metaphor representing judgmental, blame-oriented, fear-based communication rooted in survival instincts.

Globalization

The increasing interconnection of the world through trade, communication, technology, migration, and culture, producing both unprecedented cooperation and intensified conflict.

Ideology

A structured system of beliefs that interprets the world through a particular political, social, or moral lens, often offering identity and certainty in times of instability.

Inner Frontier

The unexplored territory of human emotional awareness, self-reflection, and relational intelligence.

Interdependence

The reality that individuals, societies, ecosystems, and technologies are deeply interconnected, such that the wellbeing of one affects the wellbeing of all.

Long Now

An expanded sense of time that emphasizes responsibility to future generations, often spanning centuries or millennia.

Meaning

The felt sense that life is coherent, purposeful, and significant—emerging from connection, contribution, understanding, and belonging.

Meta-Awareness

The capacity to observe one's own thoughts, emotions, and reactions without being fully controlled by them.

Myth

A shared story that provides meaning, identity, and moral orientation for individuals or societies. Myths need not be false to be powerful.

Needs (Universal Human Needs)

Fundamental requirements for wellbeing shared by all humans, such as safety, autonomy, belonging, dignity, meaning, and connection.

Nonviolent Communication (NVC)

A communication framework developed by Marshall Rosenberg that emphasizes observation without judgment, awareness of feelings and needs, and collaborative requests rather than demands.

Planetary Consciousness

An emerging awareness that humanity is a single species sharing one fragile planet with a shared fate.

Political Tribalism

The tendency to treat political identities as moral or existential tribes, often replacing religious identity in modern societies.

Regeneration

The practice of restoring, healing, and renewing systems—ecological, social, psychological—rather than merely sustaining or exploiting them.

Relational Intelligence

The ability to navigate human relationships skillfully through empathy, communication, emotional literacy, and needs-awareness.

Stewardship

The ethical responsibility to care for resources, ecosystems, cultures, technologies, and future generations rather than exploit them.

Supra-Conscious Civilization

A future form of civilization characterized by distributed intelligence, emotional maturity, compassion-based ethics, and collaboration between biological and synthetic minds.

Synthetic Intelligence

Non-biological intelligence created by humans, including AI systems that can learn, reason, and interact meaningfully.

The New Glue

The central thesis of the book: that humanity's next unifying force will not be religion or politics, but a shared capacity for empathy, needs-based understanding, and conscious relationship.

Tribalism

An instinctive pattern of in-group loyalty and out-group hostility rooted in early human survival mechanisms.

www.ingramcontent.com/pod-product-compliance
Lightning Source LLC
LaVergne TN
LVHW051824080426
835512LV00018B/2722